Praise for *The Art of Leadership*

"The best way to learn something is not to be taught a lesson—it's to be told a story. Human beings crave good stories, and Michael Lopp is a natural-born storyteller."

—*John Gruber, Writer, Daring Fireball*

"*Small Things, Done Well* is packed with real-world experience and practical actions that you can act on today to help become a better leader."

—*Cal Henderson, Cofounder and CTO, Slack*

"Lopp has delivered the book your team desperately wants you to read."

—*Michael Sippey, Chief Product Officer, Medium*

"Like watching an athlete at the top of her game, you can spot excellence, but hidden from obvious view is the winding journey of hard-earned skills that got her there. With *Small Things*, Lopp shares his leadership journey and the secret menu of tips to guide you along the way."

—*Julia Grace, Director of Engineering, Apple*

"In a sea of leadership advice which waxes philosophical and theoretical, Michael Lopp's *Small Things, Done Well* offers actionable advice you can use daily."

—*April Underwood, Cofounder #Angels and former Chief Product Officer, Slack*

The Art of Leadership

Small Things, Done Well

Michael Lopp

Beijing · Boston · Farnham · Sebastopol · Tokyo O'REILLY®

Acquisitions Editor: Melissa Duffield

Development Editors: Alicia Young, Nicole Taché

Production Editor: Katherine Tozer

Copyeditor: Rachel Head

Proofreader: Rachel Monaghan

Indexer: Judith McConville

Interior Designer: Monica Kamsvaag

Cover Designer: Randy Comer

Illustrator: Rebecca Demarest

May 2020:   First Edition

Revision History for the First Edition

2020-05-13:   First Release

See *http://oreilly.com/catalog/errata.csp?isbn=9781492045694* for release details.

978-1-492-04569-4

[LSI]

To Rachelle.

Neither I nor you,

But us.

Contents

| Foreword xi

| Introduction xiii

| Small Things xix

ACT I | Netscape: Manager

1 | Assume They Have Something to Teach You 3

2 | Meeting Blur 5

3 | The Situation 9

4 | Act Last, Read the Room, and Taste the Soup 13

5 | Spidey-Sense 17

6 | Your Professional Growth Questionnaire 21

7 | A Performance Question 25

8 | Rands Information Practices 29

9 | The New Manager Death Spiral 33

ACT II | Apple: Director

10 | The Blue Tape List   43

11 | Delegate Until It Hurts   47

12 | How to Recruit   51

13 | Gossip, Rumors, and Lies   61

14 | Rainbows and Unicorns   69

15 | Say the Hard Thing   73

16 | Everything Breaks   79

17 | The Org Chart Test   87

18 | A Distributed Meeting Primer   91

ACT III | Slack: Executive

19 | Allergic to Wisdom   99

20 | The Guard   103

21 | The Culture Creek   107

22 | Anti-Flow   113

23 | A Meritocracy Is a Trailing Indicator   117

24 | How to Build a Rumor   125

25 | Kobayashi Maru Management   131

26 | The Signal Network   137

27 | A Precious Hour   143

28 | Find a Mentor   147

29 | How to Rands   153

30 | Be Unfailingly Kind   159

| Epilogue: The Way I Heard It Was...   165

| Index   171

Foreword

Whenever I hired a new engineer at Instagram, I would tell them: "Welcome! This is now officially the biggest team I've ever managed." Scaling Instagram's engineering team from 2 to 500 in just a few years necessitated a crash course in the principles, behaviors, and habits that make for successful teams and helpful managers. During that time I was a sponge, absorbing advice from coaches, books, articles. Top of my sponge list? Reading Lopp's books and articles, and later getting thoughts from the man himself.

Those years of building out the team taught me that management is fundamentally about uncovering information—roadblocks your team is facing, interpersonal friction, etc.—and then slicing through the BS to find the right way forward. Doing it well means getting good at both of those. On the information front, it means asking the right questions and designing an intentional culture that fosters truth telling. In terms of finding a path forward, it means learning about the universe of possible solutions and then choosing the best one for the particular situation.

That's the "what"; Lopp is here to show us the "how." And the "how" is a continuous process of self-improvement built by understanding, adopting, and refining the right habits and practices—the small things, done well.

The first time you try out a new management nugget—one of Lopp's small things—it'll probably feel a little uncomfortable, like a new shirt that hasn't yet been tailored. Your team might wonder if you're trying something you just read in a book (which, in fact, you are). But you push through the awkwardness, until the behaviors become second nature, and then the magic happens where you add your own twist on them and make them your own.

I can think of no better way to build the management muscle than that. So, to my 2010 self: sorry, I wish you'd had this book. But to you, reading this now: enjoy the ride.

—*Mike Krieger*
Former CTO at Instagram

Introduction

This is a book full of small things. Simple, memorable leadership acts and practices that I've gathered and refined over the years.

Here's my favorite: I've preached 1:1s, weekly recurring meetings with direct reports, for decades. I believe a 1:1 represents the simplest and most reliable way to build trust between you and your coworkers, by providing a weekly high-bandwidth conversation on current events affecting the team. 1:1s are the first meeting I schedule when I show up at a new gig and they are the last meeting I'll reschedule or cancel during busy times. 1:1s have been my team-building go-to move for years.

Where'd this belief come from? Why do I think they're so important? I discovered 1:1s at Netscape in the mid-1990s. A recurring weekly meeting with the boss. It was a thing that managers did, but that didn't make them relevant. Just work that I was supposed to do, so I scheduled them.

Months and years passed, and I dutifully did my 1:1s. A habit? Perhaps a better term to describe what's contained inside this book would be leadership habits —small acts, repeated over time until they become second nature. There is an intersection between my list of small things and habits, but you're not going to learn from these practices just by having them become second nature.

What I discovered after hundreds of 1:1s was that these meetings presented the highest signal of the week. Real conversations about the important topics that week. Critical bidirectional conversations revealing information that I have found no other reliable way of discovering.

My belief in 1:1s, the reason I schedule them for 30 minutes, every week, no matter what, is because I've now done thousands of them. I've learned how to always productively fill the time, I know how to get the curmudgeonly engineer to appreciate them, I know what to do when they go sideways, and I have a good idea what's up when someone declines them without reason. They are a habit, but the habit isn't what taught me that 1:1s are important—it was the compounding value of the experience gained performing each one.

I learned that 1:1s are the single best way to build professional trust and respect with your team—but you won't truly believe me until you've done a couple hundred of them and seen the results for yourself.

Sounds like a lot of work, right? It is.

I originally pitched this book as a set of "leadership hacks." The title fit. Sort of. I'm an engineering leader. I am surrounded by talented engineers who often pride themselves on developing hacks. I spend a lot of time writing about leadership and packaging that wisdom, and the concept of a hack feels efficient and familiar.

Problem is: you can't hack leadership.

The term *hacker* originated at the Massachusetts Institute of Technology and is meant to describe someone who does interesting or creative work at a high-intensity level. This applies to anything from writing computer programs to pulling a clever prank that amuses and delights everyone on campus. An example: in 2009, a group of students put a half-scale model of the lunar lander on the Great Dome at MIT to celebrate the upcoming anniversary of humans setting foot on the moon.

Clever. Amusing. Not leadership.

Leadership, like any complex skill, can't be hacked; it must be thoughtfully and patiently built. Leadership is built on a set of practices, but the judgment of choosing when to use or deploy a certain habit is the art of leadership. One of the primary reasons there are not noteworthy university degrees in leadership is because leadership is a set of skills you must learn from the job.

At this point in our history as a species, we are unfortunately addicted to the idea of time-saving "hacks—simple," clever ways to quickly achieve or know a thing. This is not that book. This is a book of repeatable practices that over time will combine to form sustainable, self-improving leadership.

Pick a small thing, practice it for three months, and discover for yourself how it will make you a better leader.

Interested? Let's begin.

How to Use This Book

There are two ways you can approach reading this book: randomly or linearly. Let's talk random first.

Like in my previous books, many of the chapters of this book are standalone. Coming from decades of writing on my blog, I have a penchant for self-contained chapters. Each of these chapters contains at least one small thing. To help you pick a small thing to get started with, I've compiled a complete list of Small Things contained within the book (you'll find it after this introduction). If you're looking for help on a specific small thing, you can skim the list and jump to wherever inspiration strikes. Are your staff meetings feeling a little dull? Are you doing all the talking? Check out my tip for adding a recurring agenda topic to encourage gossip, as discussed in Chapter 13.

The linear path within this book provides a more narrative structure. The book is broken into three acts, with each section representing a key leadership stage in my career: manager, director, and executive. Each of these sections begins with a very brief history of the company where I truly learned about the role—Netscape, Apple, and Slack, respectively. The section openers also contain brief definitions and descriptions of the responsibilities of the leader as a manager, a director, and an executive.

For any given chapter, you might start it and think, "Good idea." Or you might think, "Well, that's dumb, I'd never do that." Turns out, you have the mutant power of knowing the time without ever looking at a clock. I wish I did, but I don't, so whenever I enter a meeting my first move is to turn a clock to face me so I can check the time without interrupting the flow of our meeting. Skip a chapter if it doesn't speak to you. It's fine, you won't miss part of the narrative.

While this book contains a comprehensive list of small things compiled over three decades of leadership, I'm not actively using all of them. Many may not cleanly apply to your current situation. As each company culture is different, so is each team, and each team member. Starting meetings on time is nonnegotiable in my book, but in some company cultures every meeting starts five minutes late, no matter how many times I attempt to set the tone by showing up two minutes early.

Regarding names: there are proper names throughout this book. Just about all of them are fake, with some notable exceptions for CEOs, founders of companies, and mentors. Similarly, while I attribute these lessons to my time in these companies, the stories I tell to explain them are fake.

Finally, throughout the book you'll notice I interchangeably refer to myself as both my last name (Lopp) and my online persona (Rands). The latter is a name I began using in the mid-1990s for my online presence and is predominantly featured on the Rands in Repose weblog (*https://randsinrepose.com*). The former is, well, my name.

O'Reilly Online Learning

 For more than 40 years, *O'Reilly Media* has provided technology and business training, knowledge, and insight to help companies succeed.

Our unique network of experts and innovators share their knowledge and expertise through books, articles, and our online learning platform. O'Reilly's online learning platform gives you on-demand access to live training courses, in-depth learning paths, interactive coding environments, and a vast collection of text and video from O'Reilly and 200+ other publishers. For more information, visit *http://oreilly.com*.

How to Contact Us

Please address comments and questions concerning this book to the publisher:

O'Reilly Media, Inc.

1005 Gravenstein Highway North

Sebastopol, CA 95472

800-998-9938 (in the United States or Canada)

707-829-0515 (international or local)

707-829-0104 (fax)

We have a web page for this book, where we list errata, examples, and additional information. You can access it at *https://oreil.ly/the-art-of-ldrshp*.

Email *bookquestions@oreilly.com* to comment or ask technical questions about this book.

For news and information about our books and courses, please visit *http://oreilly.com*.

Find us on Facebook: *http://facebook.com/oreilly*

Follow us on Twitter: *http://twitter.com/oreillymedia*

Watch us on YouTube: *http://www.youtube.com/oreillymedia*

Acknowledgments

My professional career would be in shambles without 1:1s—and by 1:1s I mean recurring meaningful meetings with my team. A significant number of the small things you will discover in this book were defined and refined with the talented humans I've worked with over the past decade.

I'd like to acknowledge and thank the following humans who unknowingly contributed to the creation of this book:

- Julia Grace. I have never met a human who has more drive and is also always prepared with incredibly thoughtful and penetrating questions.

- Marty Kaplan. My coach. Thank you for teaching me the importance of feedback by consistently and constructively giving it to me.

- Cal Henderson. You taught me the importance of listening to every single word being spoken and understanding those words—and, when understanding wasn't obvious, the importance of stopping everything to ask clarifying questions.

- Brandon Jackson. I have never professionally argued more with anyone. These arguments built our trust and respect, and that's when the real lessons began. Thank you, my brother.

Finally, to Rachelle, Spencer, and Claire. My family. Thank you for sitting with me at dinner and laughing. The best part of every day.

Small Things

As a Manager:

- Have 1:1s. Learn how to listen for the important signal. (Chapter 1)
- When you sign up for a thing, get it done. Every time. (Chapter 2)
- Take a measured approach to dealing with disaster. (Chapter 3)
- Act last. Read the room. Taste the soup. (Chapter 4)
- Listen for one experience that speaks loudly. (Chapter 5)
- Each month, ask yourself how you are investing in your growth. (Chapter 6)
- Have a monthly conversation with your manager to get feedback on how you are doing. (Chapter 7)
- Invest in saving yourself time. (Chapter 8)
- Let others change your mind, and tell them when they have. Build a diverse team. Delegate. (Chapter 9)

As a Director:

- Be patient when things feel broken. (Chapter 10)
- Delegate until it hurts. (Chapter 11)
- If you're hiring, spend time on it every day. (Chapter 12)
- Have a staff meeting that has weekly metrics, includes team-sourced topics, and allows the team to gossip. (Chapter 13)
- Well-timed and sincere compliments are free leadership points. (Chapter 14)

- Build a team where folks are willing to tell each other hard things. (Chapter 15)

- If your team is growing, your ways of working will constantly need to evolve. (Chapter 16)

- Draw your org chart for someone else. See if they get it. (Chapter 17)

- Invest in reducing the communication tax for distributed team members. (Chapter 18)

As an Executive:

- Act without asking. (Chapter 19)

- Build a team that understands itself. (Chapter 20)

- Listen to the stories to understand the culture. (Chapter 21)

- Protect your unstructured time. (Chapter 22)

- Make it clear that leadership can come from anywhere in the team. (Chapter 23)

- Find the truth in the rumors. (Chapter 24)

- Don't yolo the comms. (Chapter 25)

- Find and cultivate high-signal humans. (Chapter 26)

- Work to appear not busy. (Chapter 27)

- Find and cultivate a mentor. (Chapter 28)

- Write down the things you believe as a manager. (Chapter 29)

- Be unfailingly kind. (Chapter 30)

ACT | I

Netscape: Manager

THE STORY AS I HEARD IT WAS Jim Clark, founder of Silicon Graphics, wanted to do something with his money. He talked with a lot of folks and eventually found Marc Andreessen, who if you ever have a chance to meet him just reeks bright. They tried to do something with Nintendo but that didn't work out, so Marc suggested they work on the project he'd begun at the University of Illinois at Urbana-Champaign—a *web browser*, named Mosaic. It was 1994.

Most of Marc's cohorts at Urbana-Champaign were still there, so Jim and Marc got on a plane with a plan to hire them all as cofounding engineers. They mostly accepted, moved to the Bay Area, did a death march or two, and then released early versions of the browser for Windows, Mac, and Unix.

They gave this software away.

More death marches followed, as did more releases of the software on all the platforms, additional hires, more office space, the thrill of a start-up atmosphere, and eventually an IPO that changed everything.

I arrived in 1996, after the IPO, at peak hype. Not remotely my first job. I'd left the University of California, Santa Cruz, to be an engineer at Borland. After Microsoft monopolistically clubbed Borland to the brink of death I escaped to Symantec, another early Silicon Valley darling, but nothing compared to the buzz around what had become known as Netscape.

Early in my tenure as an engineer, Tony, my first manager, walked into my taupe cubicle on the second floor of the Netscape Middlefield office and asked, "Do you want to be a manager?"

"Sure."

Netscape was my fourth job in high tech. My manager at Symantec had handed me a forgettable lead position, which was defined as a path to manager.

The management role never coalesced because I bolted for Netscape as an individual contributor (IC). Thanks to the incredible growth of the company, a management role opened up for me there within six months.

Management. I was a *manager*. It seemed like important progress, but for a job so critical to the growth of a team, organization, and company, I received precisely zero training. More confusingly, it appeared the path forward was to make it appear like I knew what I was doing. "Yes, yes. I'll go talk with HR and open a req."

Wait, who is my HR partner? What is a req? What is a staff meeting? How should I run one? Why was I invited to this meeting? What is my role here? What is a performance review? How do I write one well? How much do I involve my team in the performance review process? How do I grow my team? Wait, how do I grow my team when it's unclear how to grow myself?

The book (physical or digital) you're holding in your hands is a direct result of my frustration with the lack of well-defined support during my first years of being a manager. The presumption that the optimal way to figure out the role was via osmosis and serendipity struck my engineering brain as horrifically inefficient. It was a gentleman named Tom Paquin—the first engineering manager at Netscape, who later joined me at my first start-up as a consultant—who was the first person to give me credible and useful feedback on my job as a manager. That was *five years* after I started in the role.

Paquin said to me, "Lopp, you're a good engineer, but you're going to be a great manager because you find it easy to read human beings. You understand before anyone says anything in a meeting what is going on. You know who needs what, who is mad, who is bored, and what needs to happen in the next 30 minutes to make the meeting productive. Thing is, you do this instinctively so you think it's not a valuable skill. It's an essential skill for a manager."

"Oh."

In our first act, let's adopt the following perspective: you're about a year into the new management gig. It's been long enough that you believe you know what you are doing, but you're still wondering about the importance of 1:1s, whether you need a mentor or not, how to think about managing performance...and, wow, there sure are a lot of meetings.

Assume They
Have Something
to Teach You

The daily morning calendar scrub before work goes like this:

1. Open the calendar and look at the entire day.

2. Note the number of meetings and the amount of unscheduled time. If unscheduled time is zero, die a little inside.

3. For each meeting, ask the internal question, "What do I need to do to be prepared for this meeting?" and act on the answer. Reread a spec? Glance at our Q2 goals? Make sure action items from the prior meeting are done, or just known? This is essential precaching that I don't do in the meeting because it would mean I was wasting the other human's time remembering why we're having the meeting.

4. When step 3 is complete, I'm almost done. There is one final subjective assessment that I make for each meeting: how much value is it going to create? Based on this, I can make a super-subjective estimate of how productive the day will be. This aggregate assessment allows me to determine before the day starts whether it will be one of high-energy forward progress or a morass of marginally interesting minutes.

Marginal meetings are unavoidable, and identifying them ahead of time gives me a chance to figure out an angle to increase their value. I've got one small thing that works consistently: *assume they have something to teach you.*

It works like this. Hypothetical scenario: a recruiting meeting with someone who is interested in working at my company who is a referral from a human I trust. The problem is, they want to work in a different part of the organization. While I know little about the other team, I do know there are no open jobs there and won't be for a while.

This meeting is of perceived marginal value because I'm not interviewing this person for a gig, because there is no gig. Also, I'm not qualified to interview this person because their skills are different than mine—they're on a different team. I do trust my referring friend, though, and I want to do them a solid. I know most hires are referrals. And I'm responsible for representing my company, which is why this meeting is on my calendar.

More importantly, *there are actually no marginal minutes*. It is my personal and professional responsibility as a leader to bring as much enthusiasm, curiosity, and forward momentum as possible to every single minute of my day. When I find myself in a situation where the value is not obvious, I seek it because *it's always there*.

"Hi, Cathy. How do you know Ray? Interesting. How'd you two end up working together in such different parts of the company? No way. I never imagined that legal and engineering would end up working together on that! Tell me that story?"

With three questions, I've uncovered a story that will teach me a lesson. Cathy is telling me about the time that she and my friend Ray ended up cowriting a code of conduct for their company. I've never written one, but I understand the value, and here is someone sitting here who can teach me how it's done. Splendid.

Life isn't short. It's finite. As a leader with a finite set of minutes, it is your job to find the stories and make the minutes meaningful. Find the stories—they are always there, and they will teach you.

Meeting Blur

Wednesday afternoon. 3:30 p.m. Tanya and I are walking through a complex political scenario involving product and engineering. Nothing devious. Just complex. Many moving parts. I've had some version of this conversation five times today.

The whiteboard is my savior. I'm using it to draw a picture that anchors the core points of the situation. Those core points change from conversation to conversation, and I update the picture to capture this emerging reality.

The problem is, the picture captures *my* reality, and not the reality of the people with whom I'm conversing. When it comes to complex political scenarios, you need to keep track of who knows what. Again, nothing nefarious. No ill intent. Just an honest attempt to shape the narrative productively.

Tanya says something important. Really important. It's high on the Richter scale of thought, and I need to update my entire thinking in a moment. Problem is, I've had this conversation five times today, and suddenly I cannot remember what was said by whom, when, and where.

Welcome to Meeting Blur.

Too Much

As a leader, you have disproportionate access to developments in your team and company. Nothing surprising here. You are the representative of your team, so you get invited to a lot of meetings for representatives. These meetings contain synthesized information about what is going down in the company right now.[1]

---

[1] This is why when you go to these meetings, you must report back to the team. What happened? What'd we learn? What's happening next? Everyone on your team knows this meeting happened, but only you know *what* happened. Share the knowledge. Free leadership points.

Because of your access to all this information and your disposition as a person who gets things done, you sign up for things. Often you will sign up for too many things. Because your job is to get things done, you will often be in denial about having too much to do. I want to talk about how I know I'm in this state, and the unexpectedly dire consequences.

Let's forget for a moment why there are so many meetings[2] and focus on your mental state. You're a bright, emotionally intelligent human. You walk into a meeting and have a credible mental profile of each human at the table. Why are they here? What do they want? How do they feel about the topic at hand? All of this information is front of mind and readily accessible.

This is what leaders do. We compile every single moment into a vast internal story about the state of the company. We use this informative narrative for good, not evil.

For me, Meeting Blur occurs when I can no longer compile these profiles. The amount of incoming data exceeds my ability to compile the story. *Wait? Does Tanya know this? No, Steve said it this morning, and no one else knows that thing yet. Right? Maybe...*

Blurred.

But I get things done—I've got this. This is a blur blip.

No, it's not.

If I fail to recognize my overloaded mental state at the moment, I will undoubtedly recognize it later...in the middle of the night. My eyes pop open at 3:13 a.m. and it's like I'm in the middle of meeting with Tanya. I'm compiling, I'm working on the problem, and my brain is fully engaged. In fact, it's clear that my brain has been working on the issue for some time, but at 3:13 a.m. the compilation was complex enough to wake me.

For years, I diagnosed the 3:13 a.m. wake-up call as *stress*. It is stress, but the root cause is bad leadership.

On the Topic of Operational Excellence

Let's forget about the deleterious effects of not getting enough sleep for now and talk about why Meeting Blur represents a leadership failure. You are about to

---

2 Actually, let's not. How many meetings are you having a day? How many people are in these meetings? Do they all need to be there, or have meetings become the means by which forward progress occurs? If the answer to that last question is "Yes," then you have a problem.

violate a key leadership rule: "You sign up for things and get them done. Every single time."

When you reach Meeting Blur, a reset needs to occur. Your plate needs at least one less big rock on it, and that means backing out of a commitment. Sure, you can give the work to someone else or perhaps delay another project to give yourself breathing room. There are any number of time-saving moves you can pull off, but being in this position in the first place remains a leadership failure because *you do not have a good internal measure for what you can and cannot do.*

Leaders set the bar for what is and is not acceptable on their teams. They define this bar both overtly with the words they say, and more subtly with their actions. There are two scenarios that may play out when you've reached Meeting Blur: either you don't change anything and do all of your work poorly, or you drop some of that work, which equates to a missed commitment. While the optics on both scenarios are bad, what is worse is that by choosing either course you signal to your team that these obvious bad outcomes are acceptable.

Seem harsh? Yeah, I'm a bit fired up because I think leaders vastly underestimate the impact of actions we rationalize as inconsequential. Let's play it out once more. Thinking I am being responsible and helpful, I sign up for things. I do this repeatedly and sign up for too many things. Over time, I realize I'm overloaded, so I back out on some commitments. Where's the flaw? Because I could not initially correctly assess how much work I could do, I'm signaling to my team that it's okay to back out of commitments.

What?

Yes, I am glossing over the complexity of situations that are obviously more involved. There is always situational nuance and political intrigue. There is always complexity that you discover only by doing the work. Given all of these guaranteed unknowns, a credible leader needs to be clear about one key variable: their own capabilities.

3

The Situation

Pressure's on. I can tell from the silence in the staff meeting that something is up. There is no how-was-your-weekend chat-chit, and everyone's looking around slowly, thinking about the source of the suspense. I write the agenda on the whiteboard, knowing that we're likely not going to get to any of it because...

...there's a Situation.

At some point during the past 24 hours, someone discovered the Situation. It arrived unexpectedly during a random conversation. It was delivered by a human who didn't even know they were describing a Situation. They were just the Situation carrier, but when Mateo heard it, he thought, "Smells like a Situation."

Mateo immediately took the Situation over to Erica for triage. "Situation, right?" he asked.

"Does *this* mean *that*?"" probed Erica.

"Yes," said Mateo definitively.

"World-class Situation. Red alert. You're going to need a bigger boat. Alert the troops," Erica confirmed.

Mateo triangulated the Situation with others to triple-check its Situation-ness, which is why when our staff meeting starts, no one is saying a thing. They all know about the Situation and they know when it's a verified alert-the-troops Situation, you bring it to me because as a leader Situations are my job.

I sit in my chair. I count to three. I ask, "So, what's up?"

Mateo glances at the agenda that will never be, shrugs, and says, "Before we start, I think we have a Situation."

"Describe it," I instruct.

Mateo walks through his findings and analysis. It takes seven and a half minutes and he stops to let everyone process. Beth, my second, offers a solution to the Situation and it's pretty good, but Mateo quickly points out, "This..." he pauses for effect, "...means that."

"S—t," says Beth as she falls back in her chair. Beth never swears.

After 37 seconds of silence, I ask three questions of Mateo. "If this means that, does that mean this?" *Yes.* "Every time?" *Yes, that was the first thing I confirmed and I confirmed it three times.* "Did that happen when we attempted this other thing?" *No.*

"Okay, I've made a decision. This is what we're going to do."

Everyone sighs in relief, cool air suddenly fills the room, the angels sing, and I ask, "Okay, what's next?"

Yeah...it never happens like this.

Capital-S Situations

Well, it happens like this in some situations, but never for capital-S Situations. For small situations that cross my desk, inbox, and Slack, I can dip into my experience, apply my judgment, and make a solid decision. Need justification for that decision? No problem, here's the story I've told 14 times that explains the means by which I gathered the experience to create the judgment I used in this particular situation. I am happy to tell you this story because this is how we collectively get better at our jobs: we share our experiences as stories because it's more efficient than everyone experiencing everything.

For capital-S Situations, there's no easy answer. A Situation is a complicated, never-seen-before beast, and the reason that everyone in the room is energetically quiet is that they've never seen this before and they're wondering what the hell is going to happen.

The following laborious workflow is how I make a decision regarding the Situation. Not every Situation demands all the steps. Some steps are repeated multiple times. The route through these steps varies as a function of the Situation as well as the facts, opinions, and lies I discover as I perform each step. These are the questions I ask myself:

1. *Am I the right person to handle this Situation?* Is solving this Situation truly part of my job responsibility? No? Okay, who is the right Situation handler and how quickly can I get this on their plate?

2. *Do I have complete context?* Do I have all the essential facts, opinions, and lies surrounding the Situation? Have all relevant, affected, and interested parties who care about the Situation weighed in? Have I triangulated the

facts? Have I discovered multiple different perspectives regarding the Situation? What has happened to the facts as I've looked at them through different lenses? What has this triangulation told me about my sources of information?

3. *What are the track records of my sources of information?* Do I trust the sources of information? If I have a past history with these humans, how does that color the information they've provided? Do I understand the nature of the biases of those providing the information? Am I clear on what they have to lose or gain by sharing this information? Did they acknowledge or volunteer those potential losses or gains during our discussions?

4. *What inconsistencies in facts have been discovered, and do I understand the nature of those inconsistencies?* I'm not looking for resolution of any inconsistencies, just the back story. He and she disagree on principle. They didn't have all the essential facts, so it kinda looks like they're lying.

5. *Can I coherently explain multiple perspectives on the Situation?* What happens when I explain one perspective to a neutral party? How about when I explain a competing perspective? If I can effectively explain the Situation and its complexity from both perspectives and with a distinct lack of emotion, I'm making progress.

6. *Do I understand my biases relative to the Situation?* If my role in this Situation is to make a decision, part of understanding involves understanding my bias.[1] With this understanding in mind, is there someone better placed to make the call here?

7. *Do I understand my emotional state relative to the Situation?* Emotion is sure to affect my judgment. Like my biases, it is nigh impossible to separate my emotions from an issue, whether those emotions are positive, negative,[2] or a bit of both. Am I clear on how emotion is affecting me relative to this decision? If it's affecting me negatively, will some cool-down time help? No? Okay, who is a neutral party who can make a decision here?

---

1 Easy to write, hard to do. If you want to blow your mind regarding biases, take a look at Wikipedia's comprehensive and mind-boggling list (*https://oreil.ly/Sscl7*). Start reading and tell me how long until you realize, "Uh, I do that, and I didn't know I did that."

2 I have horrific judgment when I'm mad. I'm chock-full of energy and no matter how good it feels to jump to what seems like the absolutely right decision at the moment, I'm wrong. I'm very wrong. Every time.

8. Last thing, and it's a repeat. *Am I the right person to handle this Situation?* After you've done all the work in the seven prior steps, do you still think you're the best person to decide and to act?

Capital-D Decisions

When a Situation shows up, it's full of energy. The humans are enthusiastically swirling around it, wondering "Where did it come from?" "How'd we miss this?" "How screwed are we?" and "What are we going to do?" It's easy to get caught up in the excitement, drop everything, call an emergency staff meeting, and move into wartime leadership mode.

Most Situations do not require this amount of attention. Just because the Situation arrives with great urgency doesn't mean you must always act with great urgency. The prior eight laborious steps are designed to give you context while also sending a calming dose of patience into the corporate bloodstream. *Someone is working on it. Carefully.*

There are leaders who are world class at making real-time Situation-based decisions. They stare straight into a hot burning Situation and make a call right then and there. Their track record indicates either superior judgment or incredible luck.

I'd rather be good than lucky.

4

Act Last, Read the Room, and Taste the Soup

The consistent quiet is my favorite attribute of a holiday break. My various Slacks are quiet, the house is quiet, and while it takes three days of quiet to get there, eventually my head is quiet.

Quiet enables reflection. I replay the critical parts of my recent life, and rather than living them, I observe them...from a distance. This often allows me to find the lessons rather than react to the situation.

On a recent long vacation, I found three lessons during my reflection on recent events at work. They are lessons I wish I'd learned a long time ago, and at their centers, they are all about the quiet.

Act Last

In poker, a full table is 10 players, and the betting starts to the left of the button, which is a round plastic thing to indicate the dealer. The button sits in front of one player and rotates clockwise with each subsequent hand, indicating the last player to bet. This is the prime position because you get to see how every other player at the table is going to play this hand. You have the most information with which to make a betting decision.

Oddly, at work, you will find yourself in precisely the same situation. You'll be sitting in a meeting where folks are going around the table and giving their opinion about some important topic—and for a great many situations, when it's your turn to offer your opinion, the savvy move is to pass.

Information builds context, and context is what forms the setting for an idea so that it can be understood. The more folks go around the table and weigh in with what they think about the idea, the more context you have, so the better you can shape your opinion before you share it.

Extroverted humans love to own the energy of a live conversation, which means they'll likely play their cards right out of the gate. Unlike in poker, this is often the right move to land a new idea. It's called "first mover advantage," and for the human who wants to define the narrative by landing their compelling idea first, it's a solid opening play. The thing is, acting early might set the tone, but it doesn't make an idea sound. An idea doesn't get better with agreement; it gets better with debate. It gets better when a diverse set of humans have a chance to stare at it and share their unique, informed perspectives.

So the question is, "When to act: first or last?" It's a fair question, which is why you need to...

Read the Room

My opening move in any presentation is to read the room. The slippery question I am answering for myself is, "What mood is this particular set of humans in?" Impossible to answer, right? What is the aggregate happiness or sadness of a group of 10 or 50 or 500 humans? How are they feeling? And why does it matter?

The reason you care about the ambient mood of a group of humans is that you have business with the folks—you have a talk to deliver, you have a 1:1 to complete, or you have an urgent topic to discuss at a cross-functional meeting. Their collective mood is a critical signal informing your approach path for getting your work done, and the sooner you've tested the mood, the sooner you have an approach vector.

Here are my opening moves for reading the room.

For a talk, I almost always open with an audience participation exercise. *Raise your hands. How many extroverts? How many introverts?* Why do I care about the split of perceived personality types? I don't. What I care about is how many folks willingly raise their hands. If you have five hundred people and only one hundred raise their hands to identify as extroverts or introverts? Okay, this particular crowd has its guard up. No clue why, but it means they're holding me at arm's reach, so I'll do extra work to connect by explaining my background and my goals for the talk to make myself seem more familiar.

For a 1:1, I ask, "How are you?" I listen carefully to the answer. What's the first thing they say? Do they deflect with humor? Is it the standard off-the-cuff answer? Or is it different? How is it different? What words did they choose, and how quickly did they say them? How long did they wait to answer? Did they even answer the question? Do you understand the answer isn't the point, either? The content is merely a delivery vehicle for the mood, and the mood sets your agenda.

Finally, a meeting—and to make it harder, let's say it's a meeting I am not running, but in which I have a role as a participant. Not being able to land the first question and set the tone makes the initial read harder, but all the signal I need is still in the room. Who is running the meeting? How do they open it? Who perks up? Who keeps their nose buried in their phone? As the topic changes, how does the demeanor of each denizen change? What do I know about each participant in the room, and how might that context inform my reading of their changes of mood depending on the topic?[1]

Reading the room is the specialty of introverts, because we are comforted by the act of gathering of context. This context gives us the impression that we have a map for how this particular meeting might go. But where introverts can fail is when all we do is listen, all we do is build more context, and we don't...

Taste the Soup

What do you hate about micromanagers? I'll tell you what I hate. I hate leaders who believe that prescribing every single action without room for improvisation, iteration, or feedback is anything but demeaning and demoralizing. If I screwed up, if I failed on something critical because I failed to listen to your guidance, then sure...dictator it up. Until we arrive at that failure case, I don't need to be told what to do; I need you to taste the soup.

In your career, you've had a lot of soup. You've had tomato, chicken noodle, potato and leek, and countless others. More importantly, you've had different variations of each soup. Big huge noodle chicken noodle. Some amazing type of cream on that tomato soup. This soup journey has taught you a lot about soup. Now, when presented with a new bowl of soup, the moment that counts is the first taste. You taste a bit and wonder, "What is going on with this soup?"

In a meeting where an individual or team is presenting a complex idea or project, my job as the leader is soup tasting. It's sampling critical parts of the idea to get a sense of how this soup has been or will be made. Who are the critical people? What are the critical parts? Which decisions matter? I don't know. I do believe that a prerequisite for leadership is that you have experience. You've had

---

1 Exhausting, right? Now you know why it takes three full days to clear my head.

trials that have resulted in both impressive successes and majestic failures. These aggregate lessons define your metaphoric soup-tasting ability, and when your team brings you a topic to review, it is this experience you apply to ask the critical soup questions.

Leaders who default to micromanagement teach you nothing about the craft of building. Their tell-assertive style creates an unsafe environment where some of the best parts of being human, our inspiration and our creativity, cannot exist. Tasting the soup by asking small but critical questions based on legitimate experience creates an environment of helpful and instructive curiosity. *Why did you choose this design? What is this metric going to tell us? What do you think the user is thinking at this moment?*

The opposite of quiet is noisy, and business is noisy. It's full of humans acting first, ignoring the room, and tasting none of the soup...and perhaps being annoyingly successful with each of these acts. Like all the advice you've ever received, mine is situationally useful, but it's based on what I value as a leader.

Let others share their thoughts. You never know when a great idea will appear. Understand that because you're the leader, your team is going to be less likely to contradict your idea—which is another good reason to act last.

Understand that everyone is busy living their lives, and they often bring those experiences to the conference, the 1:1, or the meeting. Their lives might not always fit neatly into the business, and your job as a leader is to read the room to understand what they need.

Demonstrate respect to the team by asking great questions. Be curious. Your experience has taught you lessons, and your questions often share those lessons better than your lectures. Plus, you never know what kind of soup you'll get to taste.

5

Spidey-Sense

You bump into James in the eighth-floor cafeteria. You haven't seen him in weeks, which is fine because while you've worked together for years, your paths are currently not intersecting.

"Hey, James."

"Hey! Long time, I was just thinking about you."

"Really, why?"

"Randy just called you out in the launch meeting. He said the project was a month behind. Everything okay?"

In your head, before James reaches the end of the statement, you already feel your response. It's not the emotional reaction to Randy calling you out, and it's not the road map implications of a month's delay. It's a feeling that you've been in this precise situation before. Randomly being thrown under the bus by a different VP. Publicly. None of his business, really. *What is he up to?* You don't know what's up yet, but it's a familiar feeling.

I'm talking about Spidey-sense.

Understanding Spidey-Sense

Spidey-sense is real-time wisdom. You build wisdom through experiences, small and large. These experiences leave you with impressions, opinions, and lessons learned. When they're shared with other humans, you'll find differences of opinion on their value. However, these different perspectives expand your understanding and teach you lessons. You observe it all—the different approaches, attitudes, emotions, and words. You continue to learn, and carefully index and file away those lessons.

As this corpus of knowledge grows, your brain discovers delicious patterns. *When situation X occurs, I often observe that the resulting situation Y, weirdly, happens a month later. Huh.* These collected, observed patterns compile nicely into judgment.[1] Over time and with practice, you become comfortable rendering a decision based on this judgment when presented with a new situation. You can explain and defend your reasoning because you've seen this scenario 42 times before. You've seen these types of humans act in this type of situation, and you understand the possible outcomes. Your decision is defensible. You can clearly explain it. Are you right? Only time will tell, but in any event you observe the results and impact of your decision, learn from it, and the cycle repeats.

The prior two paragraphs are the primary reason that universities don't offer substantive degrees in leadership. Most of the essential skills required to be an effective leader are acquired and built by deliberately experiencing the seemingly infinite number of scenarios that play out during the workday...for years.

Wait, What? That's the Small Thing? Live Life? Thanks, Lopp.

Hold on.

Spidey-sense, as I said, is real-time wisdom. At some point in processing experiences, lessons, observations, people, personalities, and words, you'll begin to apply this pattern matching instinctively...all the time. More so in leadership, because you have access to more information and will be required to use that information to make big, critical decisions quickly...all the time.[2]

Spidey-sense is not paranoia. They're related, and often Spidey-sense is the reason a human becomes paranoid, but paranoia is fueled by fear. It's an impending sense of doom that one cannot control. Spidey-sense is a sudden question in the back of your brain: *Wait, what?*

Spidey-sense is a hunch that may be discovered at any moment, when you're tasting the soup (see Chapter 4). It's your experience speaking...loudly. A moment of inspiration. Of intuition. It feels like magic because the insight arrives instantly, appears out of nowhere—and that's why you should trust it.

---

1 It's full of bias, but then again, so is your brain.

2 The colorful phrase is "S—t rolls downhill." The inversion of that statement is also true: "Fires burn faster uphill." The further you are up the organizational chart, the further you are up the hill, and the more fuel there is for the fire. Teams often successfully extinguish small fires before you ever see them, but the ones that get to you are burning, and they are burning hot and often unstoppable.

Trusting Spidey-Sense

At a prior gig, we saw unexpected attrition. The company was growing at a nice clip; our outlook was rosy, but every month there was regrettable and unanticipated attrition. As these humans left, we asked them why they were leaving, and confusingly we could not discover a pattern.

After three months, I started a spreadsheet and titled it "Spidey-Sense." At my staff meeting I explained, "This is the Spidey-sense spreadsheet. If something about someone who works with you seems off, I want you to add them to this spreadsheet. Don't think about it. Just add them. Reasons are optional. We'll review them each week."

Their stares. They were blank.

"Do you suspect burnout? Add them. Are they consistently missing 1:1s? Add them. Is something just not right? Add them."

Three names were added that week—two with good reasoning. The third's explanation was unclear. The reasoning: *Something is up, and I don't know what.*

The following week one more name was added sans explanation, and the prior third had more color. *She's bored. I can just sense it.* Okay, bored we can work with (*https://oreil.ly/OazlL*).

We maintained the Spidey-sense spreadsheet for six months. In time, all the new additions were paired with an explanation because we slowly developed a language around our intuition. We started to see the intricate patterns of burnout, boredom, personality clashes, and other performance issues. Many names were eventually removed from this list with no action on our part. Our Spidey-sense proved wrong. However, the majority of the employees we added to that spreadsheet were displaying early warning signs, and it was crucial to take proactive measures rather than reactively damage controlling. Yes, many humans still left the company, but they did so in plain sight. There were fewer surprises.

Something Is Up, and I Don't Know What

Spidey-sense is a feeling. That's why we don't initially trust it—because leadership is a well-defined set of concrete principles you follow to maximize your and your team's effectiveness.

Gross. Wrong. Yuck. Okay, there's truth in those dull words. Do choose a set of principles, and do demonstrate them via your behaviors. However, speaking as a leader for many years, leadership is equal parts following a well-defined set of principles *and* making split-second decisions in the heat of battle with little to no factual information.

Spidey-sense is a feeling. You might be hesitant to heed it because you can't tell where it came from. You might attempt to ignore it because a feeling inspired by hard-earned wisdom and one inspired by an irrational emotion feel the same. They aren't, but the only way you're going to learn the difference is by first listening, then acting.

6

Your Professional Growth Questionnaire

Do you know what time of year it is? Chances are, as you read this, it's not "performance season." For many of the companies I've worked at over the past three decades, performance season is three weeks once a year. More progressive companies have one major performance cycle per year with a minor cycle six months later to allow for one-off promotions for exceptional performance, correct errors in job leveling at hiring, and perform other performance housekeeping tasks that can't wait another six months.

Three weeks. It's the time where you write your self-assessment, gather peer feedback, perhaps build a promotion packet, and finally receive feedback from your manager in written and verbal form. The minor cycle is perhaps slightly less work. Let's call it two weeks. This means if you have a major and a minor cycle, you're talking about five weeks when it is actually performance season.

Five weeks out of 52. Chances are when you're reading this, it's not performance season.

Lies.

It's *always* performance season.

The Professional Growth Questionnaire

The following is a large set of questions I think you should ask yourself multiple times a year. Furthermore, I recommend writing down your answers to these questions each time so that you can review them at a later date, because how your answers change over time is as interesting as the answers themselves.

There are no right or wrong answers to these questions. There is no grade. The exercise is meant to stimulate thinking about your professional growth, to help you understand your level of satisfaction with your current gig, and to let you consider the possibilities of a future role. There are a lot of questions here, and answering many of them will involve deep thought. Read the whole list before answering, and don't worry about answering them all.

My expectation is that, when you're done writing your answers, you'll have at least one unexpected tangible follow-up for yourself or your manager.

Let's begin.

THE QUESTIONS

- What are your strengths? How do you know that?
- What do you need to work on? How do you know that? How are you working on this area? Is your company helping?
- When was your last promotion? How was the promotion communicated to you? What is the one thing you believe you did to earn this promotion?
- When was your last compensation increase? (Compensation = base salary + bonus and/or stock.)
- Do you feel fairly compensated? If not, what would you consider fair compensation? What facts do you base that opinion on? Have you told this to your manager?
- When was the last time you received useful feedback from your manager?
- What compliment do you wish you could receive about your work?
- Are you learning from your manager? What was the last significant thing you learned from them?
- What was the last thing you built at work that you enjoyed?
- What was your last major failure at work? What'd you learn? Are you clear about the root causes of that failure?
- What was the last piece of feedback you received (from anyone) that substantially changed your working style?
- Who is your mentor?[1] When was the last time you met with them?

---

1 My definition of a mentor is a human you meet with on a regular basis who does not work on or near your team. They are usually a more experienced neutral party who serves as equal parts sounding board and sage. See Chapter 28 for more details on this topic.

- When was your last 360 review?[2] What was your biggest lesson?
- When did you last change jobs? Why?
- When did you last change companies? Why?
- What aspect of your current job would you bring with you to a future gig?
- What is your dream job? (Role, company, etc.)
- What is a company you admire? What attributes do you admire?
- Who is a leader that you admire? What are the qualities of that leader that you admire?

Always Forward

How often should you review and revise your answers to these questions? Four times a year? Five? Your call, but it needs to be more frequently than the company's official performance season because professional growth occurs *every single day*. Most days that growth is not obvious; it's the daily set of work on your plate that is predictable and understood. No surprises. The lessons are subtle and small. Perhaps mere subtle enforcement of already-discovered lessons and values like:

"I appreciate when others are dependable."

"I am bad at estimates. I should always pad my estimates by 25%."

"People are...confusing."

Other days are special. These days present an opportunity to significantly change the course of your career. It might land smack dab in the middle of your 1:1 with your manager when they unexpectedly suggest, "Do you want to be the tech lead on this project?"

Your answer to this question—to this opportunity—isn't a simple yes or no. The answer is, "How does this opportunity fit into my broader career plan?"

Career plan? Isn't that your manager's job? Yeah, kinda. But the problem with leaving it up to your manager is that they're only going to be there for two or

---

2 A 360 is a process where a neutral party gathers feedback from all the humans in your working sphere—your managers, your peers, and, if you're a manager, your direct reports. I try to do a 360 every three years because the synthesized feedback is always revealing. Again, see Chapter 28 for more details on this topic.

three years and you are you for, like, forever. You are the most informed person regarding your career plans, which means both your analysis of and your decision about this opportunity are critical.

If you're going to say yes to the opportunity, it needs to be an informed yes. What is it about this opportunity that will allow you to grow?

A Tangible Follow-Up

These types of hypothetical career-altering moments are frustratingly infrequent. That's partly because they're usually tightly correlated with that company-approved performance season, which is just lazy management. The thesis that a predetermined performance season is the efficient forcing function for growth opportunities is absurd. Growth opportunities show up year round.

Answering all of the questions in that list will help you paint a specific mental picture of both how you feel you're doing in your current role and what you're looking to do next. Hopefully, afterward you'll have at least one tangible topic for a discussion with your manager in mind.

While it is your manager's job to identify and cultivate growth opportunities for you, forming this mental picture will help you listen carefully for opportunities that might arise at any moment and give you a better rubric for quickly assessing them.

7

A Performance Question

At some point in your leadership career, you'll encounter performance management. My first bit of advice is the hardest: don't ever let yourself think or say the words "performance management." This is impossible, but aspirational. I will explain.

My hard-earned definition of performance management is: a well-defined and well-understood workflow that leads either to an employee's improved performance or their departure.

The challenge begins the moment you say or think "performance management." From that point on, the rules of manager-employee engagement change. The natural way you interact and communicate with this individual becomes structured and unnatural because performance...it's being managed. Easygoing conversations become stilted, oddly...timed, and strangely punctuated. Smart, charismatic humans will tell you, "This is part of being a manager." These humans are right, and while there are leadership merit badges to be acquired during performance management, the ultimate badge is awarded when you act early and (now for my second bit of advice) *don't end up in performance management.*

The situations that yield performance management are as varied as the individuals involved in them, but I am steadfast in my advice: do all you can to avoid the consequential risk-averse, fear-based mindset of performance management, because once you're there, reality changes.

The Checklist Sentence

In our 1:1, you start the conversation, "Nelson has been here six months, and I don't see the sustained productivity. I'm thinking about..."

I interrupt you, which is rude, but you were about to say performance management, and I can't have that. I hold up one finger, and I ask the only question that matters: "Have you had multiple face-to-face conversations over multiple months with the employee where you have clearly explained and agreed there is a gap in performance, and where you have agreed to specific measurable actions to address that gap?"

It's a big question, and there are significant words and concepts in that big sentence that humans like to forget or ignore, so while you construct your answer I am going to call out the important points:

- *Multiple* conversations. "Rushing it" is the classic entry into performance management. For a reason that feels completely valid at the time, an eager manager decides to get real with an employee. They have one hard conversation that goes poorly, so they decide it's time for performance management.

  No. Also, *no*. Three substantive conversations, at a minimum, are needed with the employee. You need to give yourself time to explain the situation clearly, and you need to give them ample time to think about what you said and ask clarifying questions. Chances are, especially for new managers, that what you think you're saying is not what is being said or heard, especially when the message is critical feedback. The second and third conversations are essential opportunities to correct any errors in communication.

- *Face-to-face* conversations. *I gave them the feedback in an email.* No, you just sent them an email with no opportunity to debate and discuss. Feedback about performance warrants two-way communication, and when you are uncomfortably sitting there delivering complex constructive feedback, you can see with your eyeballs how they're hearing it. Email, Slack, and any other non-face-to-face mediums are avoiding the important educational work of bidirectional communication.

- *Many* months. I used to be scared of flying. Takeoffs were the worst. I had a process of counting backward by seven from an arbitrarily large number to keep my mind off of my imminent death. It distracted me, but you know what helped my fear? Flying. A lot. For years.

  Substantive changes to deep-rooted human behaviors are often necessary to correct issues with humans that lead to performance management, and that means talking about those issues. Repeatedly. In different contexts. For months.

Note

I've handily tucked my most useful advice into the middle of this chapter: *give yourself months and months to discuss a gap in performance.* Analyze it from different angles and make it about learning rather than a step on the road to performance management. This requires your feedback to be…

- *Clearly* explained. If whatever the emerging performance issue had an obvious fix, you would just say to the individual, "Hey, I asked for XYZ and got ABC. Let's debug this together and figure out what happened." You are currently not in a situation where the path forward is obvious, which is why you need to take the time to clearly explain the situation. Write it down before you say it. Ask a trusted someone to listen to your explanation and see if it resonates. Then, clearly explain the situation to your employee.

Did it work? Maybe. There's an easy way to find out.

The final clause—*agreed to a specific measurable action to address that gap*—is the most important because if the employee doesn't agree with your description of the situation, they aren't going to act. How are you going to tell if they agree? You ask.

Is it clear what I'm describing, and how we can address it? Did that make sense? Do you agree with my assessment?

When asked within an aura of performance management, these questions sound entirely different than when they are asked as part of the regular course of being a leader. The structure and formality of how I'm breaking down the performance question might give you the impression that I expect your conversation to be structured and formal. Nope, nope, nope. Your attitude and your demeanor should be that of a coach. If you've flipped the switch to performance management, your demeanor is that of the Grim Reaper, and that makes the difference between them thinking, "Oh, I get it. I know what I need to do" versus "Oh, I get it. I should be looking for a new job."

What if the employee doesn't agree with your assessment? Great. Start the discussion. *What wasn't clear? What did you hear me say? What data do I not have? How do our facts differ? Is there a different approach we could use?* You've begun a healthy and clarifying conversation where the stakes are not making a decision about whether to fire or not fire, but figuring out how to communicate and work better.

What if, after you've clarified your rationale for the assessment, they still don't agree? No problem. *Let's agree to table this discussion for today. Give ourselves a week to let the conversation percolate and pick it up next week in our 1:1. We're not on a timetable. We are simply working on a project.*

What if, after percolation, they *still* don't agree? I have to follow this path because one day you, as a leader, are going to find yourself two months into a conversation where either you're not clearly explaining or perhaps they just don't want to hear what you have to say. Performance management time, right? Wrong.

Try one more approach: write your feedback down.[1] This might feel like a formal step toward performance management, but we're still not there. We're removing the interpersonal dynamics from the situation and focusing on the words, transformed into sentences, that are delivering a critical thought. Yes, there is a smidge of formality that comes with the written word, but in my experience it also comes with a higher chance of mutual clarity.

Reality Changes

The reality is that you're always managing performance. Your very existence as a leader sets a performance bar. How you act, what you say, how you treat others, how you work, all of your attributes influence how your team performs because you demonstrate what you value as a leader.

The performance management attitude I want you to avoid is the flip-a-switch approach with your team—"Well, now it's time to get serious"—because in my experience it's manager shorthand for "How do I let this human go?" rather than "How do I make this human better?"

There are very clear, obvious, and immediate situations where you do need to let a human go—for example, if they are stealing from you, you let them go. The vast majority of the situations surrounding performance, though, are coachable. The work is complex, uncomfortable, time-consuming, and often hard to measure, but it is during these hard conversations that you become a better communicator, you learn the value of different perspectives, you build empathy, you become a better coach, and you become a better leader.

---

1 Yeah, I know I said don't deliver feedback digitally. But this is at the two- to three-month mark where face-to-face discussion isn't working yet. In the case where you write feedback down, you deliver it in a printed-out form in your next 1:1.

8

Rands Information Practices

Your most precious asset is your time, and this chapter exists to save you time. You can start adopting the following set of habits right now to give yourself hours of your life back. Equally importantly, these habits will substantially increase your productivity by reducing stress, increasing focus, and ultimately improving the quality of the things you build with your hands.

Some of these practices pay immediate time-saving dividends. Some require small, consistent investment over time to achieve the desired effect. All require discipline. Some feel destructive. Many require working counter to the intent of the apps and services you use every day, because the collective goals of those apps and services often diverge from your goals.

You will have a strong negative and opinionated reaction to at least one of the bullets in the following sections. Your strong negative and opinionated reactions are a clear sign that you care about how you spend your time, so keep reading even if you're mad.

Browser

Brace yourself. Some of these will hurt:

- Make a copy of your bookmarks and store it somewhere safe. Now delete all your current bookmarks. Wiggle uncomfortably in your chair a bit. Breathe deeply.

- Start rebuilding your bookmarks from memory a bit at a time, over multiple days. No hurry. Links to your web-based tools and critical documents belong in your browser bar. News, blogs, and other daily consumables belong in your feed reader because a browser is designed to browse, not read.

- No feed reader? Configure and pay for Feedly. Learn the keystrokes.[1]

- Install an ad blocker. Be generous about unblocking the sites you regularly visit because while it's not a fair trade yet, it's the best we've got right now.

- Pin your must-have browser tools (candidates include email, calendar, and feed reader) to your favorite browser. This will keep them handily anchored in a familiar, accessible place. Pin no more than five. Unpin a tool if you haven't used it in a week. I've held steady at four for over a year: internal email, calendar, external email, and Feedly.

- Use tabs in your favorite browser. Learn the keystrokes to create new tabs, navigate through them, and close them.

- Strive to have a single browser window open at a time. Strive to have 10 or fewer browser tabs open at any given moment. Fail at both of these objectives frequently. Don't beat yourself up, but understand that each window and tab you have open creates additive distracting undetectable stress.

- Put your bookmarks in the cloud so that they are the same on your phone's browser. Your goal is that a majority of your preferences are shared with all of your devices and desktops.

A win condition: The ability to "scrub" all your consumables in fewer than 10 minutes, and the absence of a long tail of cluttered bookmarks whose compounding/increasing stresses force you to declare bookmark bankruptcy every month and a half.

Phone

Okay. It's sitting right there. Let's work on your phone:

- If your phone allows it, flag VIPs in your contact list. If there are more than seven, you're not identifying VIPs, you're identifying another set of essential humans.

---

1 What's with the incessant "learn the keyboard commands"? The math is simple. The faster you perform each individual action, the less time it will take you to get work done. If you are touching your mouse during common work, I guarantee you could be moving faster and saving time.

- Turn on any episode of season 2 of *The Office*, sit somewhere comfortable, and turn off all noncritical notifications on your phone. Critical notifications are calls from people you know and VIP notifications. Continue to ignore the voice that tells you that you need these noncritical notifications.

- Purchase and install a spam-blocking utility, and configure it to block all spam calls and SMSs to your phone.

- Return to your comfortable place, turn on any episode of season 2 of *Parks and Recreation*, and delete any app you haven't recently used on your phone. Ignore the voice in your head that says, "I'm going to need this at some point!" Remind that voice, "Deleting the app from my phone doesn't delete this app from the universe." Repeat this phrase over and over.

A *win condition*: When you have three free minutes, you don't instinctively reach for your phone.

Email

Read your inbox with the following scrubbing protocol:

- If it's a mail you want to read, read it. Enjoy.
- If the mail is from an external (nonwork) source and you don't want to read it, do one of the following without fail:
  — If the option exists, unsubscribe from the mail. This works about as well as you would expect.
  — If an unsubscribe option does not exist and you're sure you've already attempted to unsubscribe, or you are just fed up with this mail, mark it as spam. Tell yourself this is fun.
- If the mail is from a work source and it's generated by a robot (calendar notifications, code check-ins, system notifications, etc.), spend a morning learning how to filter these notifications automatically out of your inbox into a useful place.
- If you haven't already, learn the keystrokes for your favorite email application.

A *win condition*: Using this protocol I've managed to get my work and personal inboxes to inbox zero and keep them there, every day. It took months of filter tweaking and unapologetic religious spam flagging, but for the first time in years, what I have in my inbox is mostly high-signal mails that I need, with little filtering fuss. Yes, I spend a lot of time in Slack and my inbox has much less work email than your average work inbox, but I continue to get hundreds of emails per day.

Life

I am often asked how I prioritize my time, because there is a perception that I do a lot of work.[2] First and obviously, I have precisely the same number of minutes of the day that you have. Second, I am ruthless about spending my time appropriately. One of the individual practices mentioned here might only save me 10 seconds, but that's 10 seconds multiplied by completing that action a thousand times in the next month. That's around 160 minutes, or just under 3 hours of my life.

In 3 hours, I can ride 40 miles and climb 3,000 feet. I can read a sizable chunk of my current book.[3] In three hours, I can write the first draft of this piece. It will take another two hours to finish. I don't know when that time will arrive, but I know—because I care about each minute—that it will be here shortly.

You should, too.

---

2 Productivity types: notice there's no discussion of productivity apps here. I've never met a typeface, editor, or productivity system I wouldn't try, but for the past year, the work I might have done in a productivity tool has been absorbed by the system described here, plus Slack practices. I have a 1:1 channel with everyone I meet with regularly, and we use that shared space as a mutual to-do list—and it turns out that this captures a majority of the tasks I'd normally house in a productivity app. When you combine this habit with the fact that I can use my email inbox as a lightweight to-do list because it's usually empty, I don't need a productivity app.

3 Bonus: Remove anything with a screen next to your bed. Put one book there.

9

The New Manager Death Spiral

The starting gun fires, and when the starting gun fires, you run. You're a new manager, and while the sound of gunfire is startling, you run because this is finally your chance. You've been promoted to the role of manager, you want this gig, and this is your chance to shine, so you run.

I will now explain how your good intentions and well-trained instincts are going to erode your credibility, stunt the growth of your team, and reinforce the theory that most managers are power-hungry jerks claiming all the authority and making judgment calls with woefully incomplete data.

It's called the New Manager Death Spiral and, unfortunately, I can write about it effectively because I've performed parts of it. Over and over.

BANG

What I describe here is a synthesized version of the New Manager Death Spiral. It combines every single leadership mistake you can make, spun into a beautiful, cascading, horrific mess. It is unlikely that you'll perform the Death Spiral this completely, but I guarantee that you'll perform parts of it.

It begins with a thought: "I can do it all. I'm the Boss."

As a new manager, you want to prove yourself, so you sign up for everything, you work late, and you do your very best to kick ass and make a good first impression with your new set of direct reports. This is the approach that worked well for you as an individual, so, of course, it'll work when you're leading a team. This is where the Spiral begins, because the initial thought is actually, "I can do it all *myself*. I'm the Boss."

You are used to having complete visibility and total ownership of your work because that is how it worked in your former individual contributor work life.

You are instinctively reluctant to delegate your work because it represents an unfamiliar loss of power and context. Compounding your poor judgment is your belief that you are the best person to do this because you've done it before as an individual.

The problem is your enthusiastic effort to prove yourself. You signed up for far more work than you could possibly do yourself, which leads to your first failure mode: the quality of your work drops because you lack the time to correctly complete it. Missed deadlines, dropped commitments, and half-completed work passed off as the final product are just a couple of awkward situations you stumble into.

The Spiral starts to pick up speed now because *you can see the glimmer of your failure in their eyes.* You update your mantra with an affirmation: "I can do it all *myself.* I'm in *control* because I am the Boss."

With the first admission of the reality of the situation, you begin to half-delegate the smaller, less important projects. Half-delegation is the act of giving others the work, but not full control or context. They don't need it, right? You're the Boss. You'll tell them when they need to know.

Like you, the team then starts to fail, either because they feel they don't have the authority to change the course of the project or because their lack of understanding of the full context around the project had them pointed in the wrong direction from day one. They are not on the Death Spiral, so they bring this to your attention.

First, They Tell You

This is where the Spiral gets painful. Remember, the Spiral represents every possible wrong decision stitched together.

The team working on the failing project schedules a meeting where they clearly state, "We didn't understand that this portion of the project was more important, so we started over here, which, in hindsight, was clearly the wrong place to start."

You're internally frustrated. You think, but do not say, "It's obviously the wrong place to start. If I were running this project, we wouldn't be in this situation." You're right, but you're also so wrong. You're right that if you were hands-on running this project, your prior experience would've improved execution. You're wrong because a strategy of not building trust through successful delegation is one of the greatest accelerants to the New Manager Death Spiral.

However, you cannot appear weak. Remember the line: "I can do it all *myself.* I'm in *control* because I am the Boss." Changing strategy is an admission of failure, failure is a weakness, and you are not weak because you are the Boss. You give the barest of corrective advice and tell them, "Go figure it out...or else." Of course, you would never actually *say* this, but there are many ways to get the message across. I can say this by saying nothing at all.

Your team leaves this interaction with the following impression: they are failing, and you're mad, inflexible, and unwilling to listen to their opinions. This is the point in the Spiral where they stop talking to you and start talking to each other.

Then, They Tell Each Other

Since you aren't listening, this team starts talking amongst itself and to other teams. They are trying to self-correct, and perhaps they might, but this is the Death Spiral, so they don't. They fail. This is unfortunate, because they had all the data to be successful and just needed a leadership nudge, but since it was clear you didn't want to hear it they didn't share, and the project failed.

Everyone is demoralized and everyone feels like they failed, but since no one is truly communicating, all sorts of opinions start to become facts. You tell yourself the story that you might not have the right people on the team, and perhaps if you shuffle people around you'll get a better outcome because when hasn't a reorg fixed everything? They think they failed because you didn't give them context because you were busy withholding information, being proud, and not listening.

They continue to judge, and they create their own versions of the truth about you and your leadership style. There are far more of them than you, which means that their versions of the truth spread at a faster rate than yours. Eventually, a piece of that twisted truth regarding your leadership ability arrives on your plate from someone you listen to, someone you trust, and you're shocked.

And you quietly tell yourself, "This is not *me.*"

Congratulations. Through a deft combination of poor communication, crap judgment, and systematic demoralization of your team, not only have you ensured the failure of the task at hand, but you've also irreparably harmed your relationship with your team and your credibility.

You're right, it's not really who you are. Who you are now is precisely the opposite of a leader.

Management Is Not a Promotion

You're promoted when you are successful in your current job. In many companies, the expectation is that you'll have been performing at that higher level for a period of time before you are promoted, so there's a good chance you're equipped for the new gig.

You do not start management equipped for the gig. Your first role in management is a career restart. Yes, you've acquired dealing-with-humans skills from being a part of a team, but the New Manager Death Spiral demonstrates how the very instincts that got you the new role are going to steer you in the wrong direction.

Granted, it is unlikely that you'll have performed every single step in the New Manager Death Spiral. But it is likely that as you read this chapter, at some point you nodded your head and thought, "Yup. I did that." Whether you performed one or all of the steps, the lessons are the same, and they are lessons I wish someone had given me as a first-time manager. Here are three of the most important small things:

- *Let others change your mind.* There are more of them than you. The size of your team's network is collectively larger than yours, so it stands to reason they have more information. Listen to that information and let others change your perspective and your decisions.

- *Augment your obvious and nonobvious weaknesses by building a diverse team.* It's choosing the path of least resistance to build a team full of humans who agree with you. Ideas don't get better with agreement. Ideas gather their strength with healthy discord, and that means finding and hiring humans who represent the widest possible spread of perspective and experience.

- *Delegate more than is comfortable.* The complete delegation of work to someone else on the team is a vote of confidence in their ability, which is one essential way that trust forms within a team. Letting go of doing the work is tricky, but the manager's job isn't doing quality work, it's building a healthy team that does quality work at scale.

At the heart of each small thing is the same essential leadership binding agent: trust. When you are actively listening, and when their ideas visibly change your decisions, you build trust. When diversity of opinion is valued and creates healthy debate, you create trust. When you truly delegate the work that made you a better builder, they will begin to trust you as a leader.

And that's who you want to be.

Apple: Director

THE STORY AS I HEARD IT WAS Steve Wozniak and Steve Jobs were high school friends. One liked to hack, one understood the eventual value of those hacks. Woz hacked, Jobs sold. They built the Apple I and put it in a wooden box. The reaction and reward were sufficient enough to fund the Apple II (stylized as Apple][), and that changed everything. It was 1977.

Personal computers blossomed into existence, and the world took note. IBM especially. Shocking everyone (including IBM), Jobs and Wozniak took the core ideas of Apple and built their own version of a personal computer. At the same time, Microsoft licensed IBM an operating system it did not own. Other companies cloned the IBM designs. PCs flourished. Operating systems, too.

Meanwhile, back in Cupertino, Apple stumbled with the Apple III and the Lisa. Unreliable. Expensive. From these failures came the Apple Macintosh (Mac) and a clear vision into the future, where computers would become friendly and helpful rather than a glorious impenetrable hobby.

Slow to start, the Mac gradually gathered memory and applications, becoming the default tool for poets. The IBM PCs and clones invaded business. Microsoft looked at the poetry of the Mac operating system and developed Microsoft Windows, which, as with most Microsoft products, took three major releases to become not awful.

The Mac was inspired, but it was not selling to businesses. The Apple II was. Politics, ego, and who knows what went down at Apple, and Jobs left to found NeXT. Apple was adrift and appeared to be incapable of saying no to infinite variants of the now-selling Mac.

Microsoft finally achieved Windows 3.0. The PC clones diluted IBM's market share, all powered by the increasingly dominant CPUs of Intel. Apple's flight path continued to drift aimlessly downward. Partnerships and politics resulted in

Apple acquiring Jobs's NeXT. He joined as a consultant, but we all assumed (hoped) he was in charge.

Jobs laid waste to unfocused and poorly managed projects at Apple. Some were beloved. He drew a product strategy as a box with four sub-boxes and clearly declared, "This is what we're going to do."

And they did.

Fast-forward to the turn of the century. I'm sitting at the bar at the Mexican restaurant Chevy's in San Jose with my then start-up's CEO. Getting wrecked on obscenely and unnecessarily large margaritas, we slurred through the implications of the dot-com bubble whilst planning the third round of layoffs at our failing company.

Patrick, a recruiter, called and asked, "Do you want to work at Apple?"

"I've wanted to work at Apple since I was a kid."

Steve Jobs kept teams at Apple lean and hungry. Organizational structures were as flat as possible to encourage high-bandwidth communication. Titles were not allowed, which meant no matter what you did pre-Apple, you were taking a title hit when you arrived at the Mothership.

In my case, the career optics felt strange. I'd been director at my start-up; at Apple I was a senior manager. But the role I'd stepped into was the same—I managed managers. Another uncomfortable step away from the humans doing the work.

This distance was disconcerting. As a manager, I had to deal with the discomfort of not actually doing the practical and obvious work, but at least I could glance at the engineer's monitor and get a glimpse of work happening. As a manager of managers, I had to take the word of other managers regarding how the work was proceeding. This distance is the primary challenge for the manager of managers. How do you...

- Gather and maintain context of complex projects at a distance?

- Build high-trust relationships with your team and your peers to keep communication freely flowing?

- Define the vision and strategy for an entire organization rather than a team?

- Communicate that vision and strategy?
- Adapt your organization to deliver that vision and strategy, or build an entirely new team to do so if necessary?

You know. The simple things.

Just as the role of manager is preparation for being a manager of managers, the role of director is preparation for being an executive. I spent over eight years in various manager-of-managers roles at Apple. At the time I felt I wasn't progressing quickly enough, but as it turned out, it was just right.

In our second act, your perspective is that of a seasoned first-line manager who has recently moved into a senior management position. You've figured out the leadership role, but now it's time to up your game. Politics, the good and the bad, is now part of your daily diet. Communication downward and upward has always been important, but now you must communicate sideways—and now it's time to give away your Legos.

The Blue Tape List

We remodeled the downstairs of the house several years ago. Two rooms had walls moved to make way for additional rooms. This was deep construction. Months of noise, plastic tarps, dust, and decisions.

When they start applying the drywall, it starts to look like your house again, and you begin to hope for dustless silence. Drywall is when you start wondering, "Are they going to fix that?" You spot defects. Partly completed work. Small dents. Dings. As you begin to finish, you can see everything that is not quite right.

When we brought these concerns to our general contractor, he whipped out a roll of blue painter's tape and gave us the following instructions:

1. You are going to see everything that is wrong with our work from now until we're done. That's fine.

2. When you see something that needs attention, mark it with this blue tape.

3. We will fix everything that has the blue tape.

Everything Is Broken

Our ability to see imperfections after significant context switches is impressive. A new home or remodel, a new car, a new job. When the context around you changes massively, your brain moves to high alert. *Everything is different. Pay close attention. Something important is up.*

Why? I used to think this hyperawareness was a reaction to significant expenditures; it was there to make sure I was getting my money's worth, or per- haps it was an unrealistic desire to keep what is new in perfect condition. That makes sense for big-ticket items, but why do I have the same heightened things-have-changed and this-is-wrong consciousness with a new job?

Ninety days is how long I believe it takes to understand a new job. There's a one-month honeymoon, followed by a one-month dip of despair where the shine comes off. It is during this second month that everything—large and small—that is broken, odd, or weird about the new role will jump out at you, and your brain will attempt to convince you that you've made a horrible choice by accepting it.

Look at everything that is broken. I made a mistake.

Why is the reaction to a big purchase and a big job change similar? It's the change of context. I knew how the prior room felt, I knew how the previous car drove, and I understood how the previous job worked.

Having been through this experience many times, I've discovered that a simple fix is patience. In time, that which is different will feel normal. It's why when a team member reports moderate concerns with a new hire, I always gently ask, "When did they start?" If the answer is less than two months ago, I suggest, "If it's not heinous behavior, give it another month. They're still adapting to a new environment, and we don't know who they are."

That might be good advice for a manager with a new direct report, but when you're the direct report, when you're in the middle of the second month and it all feels broken, "Just a wait a bit longer" is unhelpful advice. It's also bad advice.

You need blue tape.

A Spectrum to the Broken

Our contractor fixed everything that we marked with blue tape. It was immensely satisfying knowing that whenever my wife or I blue-taped something, it'd be fixed. In a job context, I have a modified and simplified version of my contractor's blue tape advice:

1. In a new context, you're going to notice everything that feels off.
2. Make a list of everything that feels off, no matter how big or small.
3. Wait a bit, like a month, but address everything.

You will notice my advice to new hires does not commit to *fixing* everything that feels off, but rather commits to *addressing* it. This could mean fixing the issue, but it could also mean responding and clearly explaining my reasoning why I didn't think fixing the issue was the right move.

It's a surprise when a month passes, and you review your blue tape list and discover how many items that seemed urgent at the time now seem entirely irrelevant. You are learning so much every single minute of a new gig; you are gathering so much context. You are continually updating your understanding of the team, your role, and the company. The context you've acquired after three months of work isn't remotely complete, but it is exponentially more complete than at the end of month two.

Address every item on the blue tape list. Make sure every item gets a response. If you're planning on fixing the issue, explain how and when. If you're not planning on fixing it, explain why. If you aren't sure about the issue's relative importance, think about how you might find it.

A large context shift is uncomfortable. It's an emotional time, because that which was daily familiar is now wholly foreign. When your brain defaults to high alert, it's stressful, but it's through this lens that you're able to see defects the old guard can no longer see.

All you need is a little blue tape.

Delegate Until It Hurts

I have this list. It's a list of leadership merit badges. You acquire one of these badges when you complete a task that requires significant leadership. Acquiring the badge is the least important thing. The most important thing is that you discover the lesson that awards it.

As you might expect from the structure of this book, there are three classes of badges: ones earned from the tactics of being a manager, ones earned from your strategic stylings as a director, and, finally, the slippery merit badges associated with your visionary quest as an executive.

Where can you find the complete list of merit badges? Sorry, that's another book. For now, here at the beginning of Act II, I'm just going to tell you about one of them. It's the most important leadership merit badge, regardless of role: *Delegation.*

Entrust

Let's start with a definition. Delegate. Verb. *Entrust (a task or responsibility) to another person, typically one who is less senior than oneself.* The key word in that definition is "entrust," but before we unpack that let's first step back in time to those heady first days as a manager.

Perhaps the most confusing part of the early days of leadership is the shift in responsibility. You had something that you were responsible for: an area, a feature, a technology...but now it's more. Your responsibility encompasses all of the responsibilities of all the folks on your team. As I wrote in Chapter 9, your instinct in these early days is that all the work of all your team members is your responsibility, which, while partly true, is a slippery slope.

It is true that if something were to go sideways with one of your teams, leadership will be staring at you and looking for answers. When they're staring, it sure feels like you're responsible. But a far more productive mindset is that you're *accountable*.

While accountability implies responsibility, there's an important distinction: accountability requires a willingness or obligation to justify (account for) actions and decisions. This means when it goes sideways and everyone's staring at you, you need to be able to explain both how you got there and what is going to be done to fix it. How do you know these things? Your team has already told you... voluntarily.

When things go sideways, when the sky falls, you'll rush to find the humans who know about the problem area. They know you're in a dire situation and they know you are moving with great urgency. They have a professional irrational fear and they are listening to *every single word you say*.

At this moment, a manager who believes they are solely responsible for this situation will say "I" a lot. They are going to ask penetrating questions that indicate it's *their* problem to solve because important people are asking them hard questions. They feel responsible, and hidden between the words they use and tucked nefariously behind the questions they ask is the distinct impression that they believe *If I were the engineer running this, we would've never ended up in this situation.*

Watch trust erode.

The reason Delegation is the most important merit badge is that earning it means you've learned important leadership lessons that will allow you to accelerate your leadership journey.

Shush, Little Voice

Your VP gives you a new project. It's work that you, as an individual, have done many times. It'd be a slam-dunk project if you were doing it solo, but you're a director with no time to code, so you hand the project to one of your managers, Julie.

At your 1:1 with Julie, you explain the project. You walk her through what winning looks like with this project, you talk resourcing, and you talk scheduling. Julie has never done anything like this, so she asks lots of questions. You have, so you're able to give complete and informed answers. Julie scribbles your answers down and asks more questions. She's learning.

Thirty days into the 90-day project, you're hearing some concerns from the team on how this project is going. You mention to Julie that you'd like to discuss the project's status at your next 1:1. She comes prepared. She's heard the worry too, and has ideas on how to address the concerns.

Her ideas are well intentioned, but wrong. This is fine. She's never done this before. You discuss a different direction. She's quiet because she now understands her intuition was wrong, but your reasoning seems sound. She asks questions, which indicates she's adjusting her mindset.

As the project winds down, it's clear the final product is a B. It functions, schedules were met, but there are going to be performance issues with it shortly that require another month of unplanned work before the next release. It's a B.

A little voice in your head says, "If it had been me banging on the keyboard, it'd be an A." Shush, little voice. Allow me to tell you why a B in this case is credible leadership.

First, Julie knew this project was going to be a stretch for her and the team because they'd never done anything like it. You demonstrated trust by giving them this work, even though everyone knew it was beyond their means.

Second, when the project got bumpy, you didn't overreact. You sought understanding, and you coached them through it by telling them stories of the time you did this work. More trust.

Third, you've learned a valuable set of lessons on how to not be a micromanager. You gave Julie lots of initial guidance, you answered her questions, and then you let her and her team run with it. When it went sideways, you didn't punish, you coached.

Fourth, they did it. They completed the project. They delivered it and earned valuable experience in doing so. How'd it go for you the first time you did this type of work? I know I likely screwed it up in heretofore unimaginable ways. In this situation, you've increased the probability that the next project done by this leader and this team has every chance of being an A.

The complete delegation of familiar work to another human is a clear vote of confidence in their ability, which is one essential way of forming trust within a team. Letting go of doing the hands-on work is a tricky and nonobvious win, but as a leader, you build yourself by building others.

An Essential Leadership-Scaling Function

Another reason Delegation remains my essential leadership merit badge is because it is a skill that scales. You'll need one version of it as a manager and you'll need another as a director. Even better, the more advanced versions of delegation require the development of advanced skills on your side.

Here's an excerpt from a leadership career path I wrote at a prior company. This is how I describe the act of delegation at different levels of experience:

- *Manager*: Identifies and delegates small, well-defined projects to individuals within the team who require significant oversight.

- *Sr. Manager*: Identifies and delegates significant projects to individuals within the team who require some oversight.

- *Director*: Identifies and delegates large projects to teams or individuals who require little oversight.

- *Sr. Director*: Identifies and delegates large and complex projects to teams or individuals who require little oversight.

- *Executive*: Identifies and delegates large and complex projects to cross-functional internal or external teams that require little oversight.

You can see the three skills that you are developing as you grow as a leader:

- Measuring the amount of oversight provided to the team/individual
- Assessing the magnitude and complexity of projects
- Considering the composition and size of teams capable of doing the work

A common complaint I hear about managers is the classic, "What do they do all day?" You know what a good manager is doing? They're giving away just about everything that lands on their plate to members of their team because their job isn't building the product, their job is building a team that is capable of building the product.

It's confusing and challenging because you're giving away the work that likely made you...you. That work you did gave you the experience to become a better leader. Delegation isn't just how you'll scale yourself—it's how you'll build leadership within your team.

12

How to Recruit

From a recruiting perspective, the best engineering manager I've worked with established her reputation with two hires. It went like this:

> ME: "We need to build an iOS team, and while we have talented engineers, we don't have time to train the current team on iOS. It'll be faster to hire."
>
> HER: "Great, who should we hire?"
>
> ME: "Here's the perfect profile. We'll never get him, but he's an incredible, well-known iOS engineer who is not only productive but also a phenomenal teacher. He'd be a perfect seed for the team. We need an engineer like him."
>
> HER: "Why not hire him?"
>
> ME: "You'll never get him. Everyone is throwing everything at him."

Three months later, the long-shot hire that I thought we had no chance at getting signed an offer letter. Two months later, same story. I mentioned an unattainable hire, which was followed promptly by the hiring of that specific engineer.

You probably think there was some trick here. You may think we threw huge amounts of money at these engineers—we didn't. Standard compensation packages. You may think we promised them an impossibly cool role—we didn't. The offer was to build the first version of an iOS application with a talented group of engineers.

There is no trick other than carving out time every single day to do the job of recruiting.

First Rule of Recruiting: Give It 50%

Let's start with the rule. For every open job on your team, you need to spend one hour a day per req on recruiting-related activities. Cap that investment at 50% of your time. No open reqs? There's still important and ongoing work you need to do on a regular basis that I'll describe later.

Take a minute to digest that prior paragraph, because it might be a shock to many engineering managers out there. Seriously, *50% of my time?* Yup. *But we have a fully functional and talented recruiting organization.* That's super and will make your life better, but devoting 50% of your time to recruiting still stands. Why? I'm glad you asked.

On the list of work you can do to build and maintain a healthy and productive engineering team, the work involved in discovering, recruiting, selling, and hiring the humans for your team is quite likely the most important you can do. The humans on your team not only are responsible for all the work the team does but also are the heartbeat of the culture. We spend a lot of time talking about culture in high technology, but the simple fact is that culture is built and cared for by the humans who do the work. Your ability to shape the culture is a function of your ability to hire a diverse set of humans who are going to add to that culture.

Let's dive into this in more detail.

A Recruiting Primer

A good way to think about your recruiting work is to delve into the stages of the recruiting process itself. Figure 12-1 is a snapshot.

This is the hypothetical funnel chart for The Rands Software Consortium, and we're hiring![1] I love funnel charts because they help frame multiple lenses of information in a single digestible view. The stages here are:

Applications
 Applied for a role or were sourced by an internal or external party.

---

1 Not really. This is fake data, but it's fake data based on experience. I'm making a couple of assumptions regarding this fake company. It's got around five hundred employees. It's in hyper-growth, which means it has a hundred plus open reqs. Your company or team is likely in a different stage of growth, but much of the strategy of this piece still applies.

Screens

Made it past a first-round screening process.

Qualifies

Made it through a more critical screening process. Think coding challenge or technical phone screen designed to gather more signal.

Interviews

Entered the formal interview process.

Onsites

In the building for an interview.

Offers

Received an offer.

Hires

Accepted their offer.

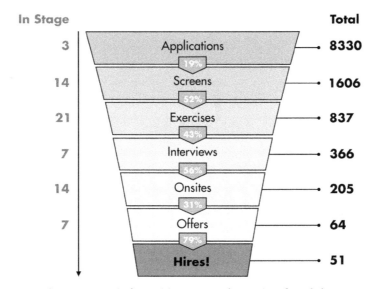

Figure 12-1. Typical recruiting process, shown via a funnel chart

This fake graph represents a period of roughly six months. The "In Stage" number shows you how long on average a candidate spends in each stage in days. The gray percent numbers down the middle show you what percentage of candidates make it through a stage, and the "Total" number on the right shows you the total number of candidates per stage in the period in question.

Before we talk about where you should be spending 50% of your time, you first need to make sure you have two agreements in place with your recruiting team:

1. Agreement on the stages in your pipeline. The fake chart shown here is just one example; your flow might be different. What are the different stages? How does a candidate enter and exit a specific stage?

2. With #1 defined, you now need to agree to make it ridiculously easy to access this information.[2]

With all this data in place and the process running smoothly, you can learn about the efficiency of the different parts of your recruiting process and you can ask informed questions. *Where are candidates spending the most time, and why? We gather the most signal at the coding exercise and the interview—shouldn't those pass percentages be lower? How long is a candidate spending in each part of the process? Is that the experience we want them to have?*

This chapter assumes you have a fully functional and talented recruiting team. These humans are essential for you to effectively do your part of the recruiting gig. Part of their job is to provide a clear and consistent perspective on the health of the entire recruiting funnel, as well as the status of any candidate in any stage in the pipeline. This partnership and this data will enable you to better understand where to invest your time.

Discover, Understand, and Delight

This chapter is not about the traditional recruiting pipeline and the familiar work you're already doing. It's about the work of recruiting you are *neglecting*. Let's call this the *engineering recruiting pipeline*—it's a pipeline built right on top of the funnel I described in the previous section. The different states in the engineering recruiting pipeline are based not on how we measure candidate progress, but on *the evolving mindset of the candidate traversing the process*. There are three states I consider as part of this unique pipeline: Discover, Understand, and Delight.

---

2 This is usually where this process comes crumbling down, because you're busy building the product and recruiting is busy recruiting, and providing ridiculously easy-to-access recruiting information requires a rigorous process supported by flexible tools. My advice if you're building this for the first time is to assign a couple of engineers to this project for a year.

DISCOVER

Discover, first, is the state of mind of any qualified candidate who does not yet know about the opportunity on your team and at your company. It is your job to find these humans and help them discover the desire to work with you at your company.

In recruiting parlance, those who find these candidates are *sourcers*. Their job is to look at your job description and identify humans who fit the bill. Sourcers cast their nets very wide and fill the top of the funnel with as many qualified candidates as possible. Sourcing is also your job during Discovery, but your time can be more focused because you have intimate knowledge of the gig. More importantly, you have likely worked directly with humans who you know can do the job. You can operationalize this fact by building The Must List.

The Must List

Make a list of each and every person you've worked with who you want to work with again. You *must* work with them again. Fire up a blank spreadsheet and start typing, because you're going to want to capture a bunch of different data, and as the list grows, you're going to want to slice and dice it in different ways.

List every person. Doesn't matter if they're an engineer or not. Keep typing. Doesn't matter if they're available or not. Write down their name, their current company, their current role, and why they're on the list. Done? Put it away for a day and then come back. You missed important humans.

There are two use cases for The Must List. First, whenever a new gig opens up on my team, I fire up the List and see if there is anyone on it who might fit the bill. Then I send them a friendly note. *Hi. How are you? Got a gig and I must work with you again. Coffee?* More often than not, if we haven't spoken recently, this human and I will get coffee regardless of their interest in the role because *these are dear friends*. Much more often than not, they are happy in their current gigs. Sometimes they'll know folks who might fit the bill. Rarely, very rarely, they'll come in for an interview. When coffee is done, I update the remaining columns in the spreadsheet: last contacted date, current status, next steps, and notes that capture their current context.

The second use case for The Must List is my monthly review. Every month or so, whether or not I have a relevant open gig on my team, I review the list and see whom I have not spoken with in the last 90 days. Time for an email? Okay: *Hi. How are you? Coffee?* Again, they're rarely interested in switching gigs, but if they happen to be looking, I will move mountains to work with them again.

Return on time invested in the Discover state is going to feel a lot lower than in the forthcoming Understand and Delight states because it's hard to measure progress. There are currently 42 humans on my Must List, and if I get one of them in the building a year, I'm giddy. However, these are my people and the time spent investing in this network almost always pays unexpected dividends in ways that have nothing to do with whether I can hire them. These are my people, and they know other people who might fit the gig or whom I should simply meet. They observe the world in interesting ways, and I want to hear those observations.

In Discovery, you are making targeted strategic investments in your network. The reason these folks are on your Must List is that you have seen with your own eyes the work they can do. You built a bond with these humans in a prior life, and these small investments of your time strengthen and reaffirm that bond. The value of this network is a function of the number and the strength of these connections.

UNDERSTAND

On to the *Understand* state. A candidate has passed through the very crowded top of the funnel and has reached the evaluation portion. If you look at the hypothetical funnel numbers in Figure 12-1, this candidate is statistically unlikely to make it to the Offer stage. But regardless of whether they end up getting an offer or not, your job is to Understand.

The recruiting focus here is, "Do they have the necessary skills?" The interview process is designed to gather this information from the candidate. Your focus during Understanding is to again consider the candidate's mindset. While they are getting peppered with questions about their skills and qualifications, they are also wondering, "Who is this engineering team?" "What do they value?" and "Where are they headed?"

Homework. Step away from your digital device this moment and ask a random engineer who is a part of your interview loops those three questions. Done? Now do it with another engineer. How do the answers compare? Is it the same narrative? Is it a compelling narrative?

The explanation of an engineering team's culture is usually left to happenstance—the last few minutes of an interview, where you ask the candidate, "Do you have any questions for me?" This lazy question is cast out with the hope that the candidate responds with a softball like, "What's it like to work here?" You respond with your well-practiced recital of "I love it here!" and "We're solving hard problems!" which sounds about as interesting as it reads.

Your responsibility is to make sure the candidates understand your mission, culture, and values.[3] While they will organically pick up some of this during interviews, you need to make sure it's one person's responsibility to clearly tell the engineering story. This is not an interview; the point is to clearly explain the shape of the place where they might work. And—bonus points—you are going to organically learn about them during the discussion of the character of your company.

There are two scenarios for a candidate passing through the Understand state. Scenario A: they receive an offer, and the time spent in Understanding paves the way to a rich offer conversation and allows them to hit the ground running when they arrive. Scenario B: they don't get an offer, but they leave with a clear understanding of you, the character of your team, and your mission. Recruiters call the time spent interviewing "the candidate experience," and I would suggest that whether they get an offer or not, Understanding is the cornerstone of an exceptional candidate experience.

DELIGHT

We've reached the *Delight* state. Congratulations! You're making an offer to an engineer. Going back and looking at those funnel ratios, you can see this is a statistically unlikely event. Let's not screw it up, okay?

New managers often erroneously think when making an offer, "We've made a hire!" Experienced managers and recruiters know, "They're not here until they are sitting in that chair." If you and your recruiting team have done your work, the presentation of the offer is a formality because you already know the candidate's life situation and goals. Offer construction, presentation, and negotiation is a topic for a whole other chapter, but it's a clear sign that you missed critical information somewhere in the candidate experience if the negotiation process is unexpectedly laborious or littered with surprises.

They accept! Hooray! We're still not done because *they are still not sitting in that chair.* Let's welcome them. Let's Delight them.

The nightmare scenario is a candidate declining an offer they already accepted. I think it's professionally bad form, but it happens more often than you'd expect. Put yourself back in their shoes: they likely have an existing gig where everyone knows their name and they know where the good coffee lives.

---

3 Yes, this means you've defined your mission, culture, and values and everyone agrees with these definitions.

Even after a phone screen, an at-home coding exercise, a day-long round of interviews, two more phone calls, and assorted emails, you and your engineering team remain an unknown quantity. In the middle of the night, when the demons of doubt show up, you represent an uncertain future—and your job during Delight is to help them imagine their future with you.

Reflecting on my experience in this state, I think of how I act after I've accepted an offer. After the initial high of receiving and accepting the offer passes, what do I do? I reread the offer letter. I review the benefits. I go to the company website and *I examine every word.* What am I looking for? Why am I continuing to research? I'm vetting my decision.

The offer letter is an important document. It contains the definitive details of compensation and benefits, and these are important facts—but during this critical time of consideration, I want these future coworkers delighted with a Real Offer Letter.

I send the Real Offer Letter a week before the start date. I write a note each time that captures the following:

1. My current observations of the company, the team, and our collective challenges.

2. The first three large projects I expect the new hire to work on, why I think these projects are important, and why I think the new hire is uniquely qualified to work on them.

3. The growth path for the new hire, explained as best I can.

Nothing in this letter should be news. In fact, if there are any surprises in it, there was a screw-up somewhere earlier in the funnel. The purpose of this letter is to acknowledge that we are done with the business of hiring, and now we're in the business of building.

During the post-offer-acceptance time, most companies send a note...a gift. I've received (and appreciated) flowers, a terrarium, and brief handwritten notes. Thoughtful gifts, but small thoughts. At a time when a new hire is deeply considering a change in their career, I want them chewing on the big thoughts. I want them to understand the humans they are joining and their mission. I want them to concretely understand what they will be working on, and I want them to understand the potential upside this new gig represents for their career.

Circling Back to 50% of Your Time

The work of recruiting is a shared responsibility. Yes, you can be a successful hiring manager devoting less than 50% of your time to it. Yes, all of the funnel work can be completed by a recruiter; many of my best recruiting moves came from watching and working with talented recruiters.

The situation I want to avoid is a hiring manager who delegates the entire recruiting process to their fully functional and talented recruiting team. There are critical leadership skills you need to learn and refine during the Discovery, Understanding, and Delight stages. In Discovery, it's understanding the power of persistent serendipitous networking. In Understanding, it's understanding how to tell the tale of your company as well as being able to understand the tale of the candidate. Finally, in Delight, it's the ability to discern the best way to delight this candidate at a time when their worry and risk aversion are the strongest.

Recruiting and engineering must have a symbolic force multiplication relationship because the work they do together—the work of building a healthy and productive team—defines the success of your team and your company. That's worth your time.

13

Gossip, Rumors, and Lies

Everyone is just...sitting there.

Six of you. All managers who report up to Evan, your boss, who decided two weeks ago that "It's probably a good idea for this leadership team to get together on a regular basis and talk about what's up." He dropped an agendaless, 60-minute recurring meeting on everyone's calendar, and that meeting is now.

Six of you. You know these humans. You work closely with two of them every single day. You've collaborated on occasional projects of significance with two others. The last two are friendly first names you see in the hallway.

Evan kicks off the meeting by repeating exactly what he told each of you face-to-face and in the meeting invite. It's probably a good idea for this leadership team to get together blah blah blah. He finishes his bland opener and everyone is just...sitting there. Saying nothing.

Welcome to your first staff meeting.

An Unacceptable Amount of Crap

I'm solidly on the record as believing 1:1s are the most important meeting of the week. A very close second is the staff meeting. I find that 1:1s beat staff meetings in two important categories: trust building and quality of signal. There are ongoing, compounding benefits to a regular well-run staff meeting, though: team building, efficient information dissemination, and healthy debate are three I can think of off the top of my head. There are more.

Definitions first. I define a staff meeting as "the correct collection of leadership gathered together to represent a team, product, company, or problem." Lots of words. A simpler and perhaps more immediately applicable version is, "a meeting of your direct reports."

Great! You have directs, which means you should have a staff meeting, right? Maybe.

The decision to start your first staff meeting requires judgment. Ask yourself the following questions:

- How many direct reports? Two? Yeah, no staff meeting necessary. Three or more? Keep reading.

- How many of your directs spend time working together? If it's more than half, consider a staff meeting.

- Do your directs have direct reports who are managers? Then you needed a staff meeting a while ago.

- How much has your team grown in the last six months? More than 25%? Have a staff meeting.

- How much of the crap that you've dealt with in the last month smells like it could have been resolved if people on your team were just talking with each other? If the amount of crap is unacceptable to you, have a staff meeting.

- Did something recently organizationally explode? Have a staff meeting. No need for it to be recurring, yet.

A Well-Intentioned Hatred of Meetings

A first staff meeting is understandably a pretty quiet affair. It's a delightful combination of unfamiliarity combined with a well-intentioned hatred of meetings. In our hypothetical opening example, Evan set a horrible initial meeting tone because he committed the worst meeting sin: no agenda.

Before I dive into these agenda topics, let's talk about two essential meeting roles. In a well-run staff meeting, 95% percent of the activity is healthy conversation and debate. Key word: *healthy*. It's a clear signal that a staff meeting is working when the majority of attendees jump into conversations and drive those conversations in unexpected directions. It's a clear sign that no one is curating those conversations when those unexpected directions are not revealing insight or value. It's time for a Meeting Runner.

The Meeting Runner has two jobs: set the agenda and manage the flow. We'll talk agenda shortly, so let's first talk about managing flow. The Meeting Runner is responsible for making the following call throughout the meeting:

When is this particular conversational thread no longer creating enough value? It's a nuanced job, but without this human curating the conversation, a staff meeting can turn into a directionless heated venting session. Fortunately, as we'll learn shortly, the Meeting Runner has an essential driving force at their disposal—the agenda.

The role of Meeting Runner is traditionally filled by the human who called the meeting. It's usually the person accountable for the team, which allegedly gives them the context to run the meeting efficiently. Usually.

The second role is Meeting Historian. This nonobvious role is not required in the first few get-to-know-you meetings, but is essential in the long term. Their job: *capture the narrative of the meeting.* We're not looking for every single word, we're looking for major themes and points that are discussed. Action items, relevant thoughts, jokes; it's all captured by the Meeting Historian.

Two guidelines for the Meeting Historian. First, it can't be the Meeting Runner because this human has their hands full keeping the meeting pointed in the right direction. Second, the Meeting Historian is not responsible for editorial direction or curation. Their job is to capture everything. This seems like a no-brainer until you understand that your next job is to send these notes to the entire company.

Wait. What?

Humans have complicated relationships with meetings. If they're in the meeting and it's not meeting their expectations, they're mad. If they're not invited to a meeting where they believe they should be present, they're mad. Combine this slippery situation with the fact that meeting efficiency devolves as a function of the number of humans greater than seven that are present, and you've got a maddening set of complicated constraints. The simple but perhaps controversial practice I recommend is that every single meeting have a Meeting Historian, and the work of that Historian be broadcast to the whole company.

If you're a frequent meeting denizen and the hair on the back of your neck stands up when you imagine the notes of your meeting being shared with the whole company, my question is, "What are you talking about in that meeting that can't be shared?" Of course, the Meeting Historian will remove confidential information about individuals as well as other clearly confidential company information before sending their summary. If that doesn't calm you down, I'm still curious what you think is being said in this meeting that can't be shared with your team.

Meetings create power structures. Intentionally or not, they become a measure of status. *Are you in that meeting? No? Well, I am.* If you found sound reason to have a staff meeting in the list given earlier, I'm not worried about the first three months of this meeting's existence. It's during year two, when that good reason may have vanished and now you have this formerly important meeting purely out of habit, that things get tricky.

The rule is: in the absence of information, humans fill the gap with the worst possible version of the truth. Two years into your meeting when you're not sharing the notes, the humans not in the meeting will be telling the most interesting and untrue stories about what happens in it. I guarantee it. This isn't out of spite. They aren't being malicious. They just don't know what's going on, so they're going to tell their version of the story.

Share your notes. Every time. The act of doing so will force you to ask the following question before you share them: "Is what we are doing here valuable?"

A Three-Point Agenda

Here's a starting agenda:

- The Minimal Metrics Story
- Rolling Team-Sourced Topics
- Gossip, Rumors, and Lies

The *Minimal Metrics Story* is the list of essential metrics this group must review on a regular basis, and I recommend leading with them because they frame the whole meeting. Not knowing precisely why you chose this exact time and set of circumstances to start holding a staff meeting makes it tricky to recommend what types of metrics you need to review.

What are the key metrics this group is responsible for? Revenue? Application performance? Security incidents? Number of critical bugs filed? The list is endless, and it's okay if your first meetings don't have them clearly defined. But after a month, if these haven't shown up, I'd be wondering why you pulled this group together. What problem are you trying to solve? I'm not saying you demonstrated poor judgment by calling the meeting, but if a concrete set of measurable things to review hasn't shown up, why is the group meeting on a regular basis?

You'll know you've found a good initial set of metrics when they tell a story and leave you with questions. *Total billings in the last week were X million. Recurring revenue added was Y thousand. The week before they were A and B? That's a big change. What do we think happened?* The questions and debate that surround the story both align the room and frame the rest of the conversation. There will be weeks where the metrics story is, "Tracking. Nothing to discuss," but if it's been three months and that's the only story, you've either got the wrong metrics or the good reason to have this meeting has passed.

A *Rolling Team-Sourced Agenda* is the heart of your meeting. For the first iteration of this meeting, you'll need to build the agenda yourself. This shouldn't be hard because there's a pressing reason for these humans to be together. Once, twice, or perhaps three times you can set the agenda for the meeting to address that pressing reason, but at the end of each of these meetings you should say, "Here's a document I've shared with everyone. Please add any agenda topics for next time."

They won't.

The social fabric and the sense of team that you are building with this meeting will take time to form, and you'll need to be more involved in both building the agenda and moving the narrative along for the first handful of meetings. You're looking for two important developments over the course of the first three meetings:

- Unexpectedly useful conversational detours. You're going to do a lot of talking in the first few meetings because you're the leader, you've identified some problem, and you're attempting to solve it. Good job—but very quickly you need to stop talking. The introverted leaders of the world will have no problem with this advice. Extroverted leaders, listen to me. It's not your meeting, it's their meeting. You need everyone in the room to bring their experience, their questions, their curiosity, and their drive to the table, and they each need to feel comfortable sharing their thoughts. If you don't stop talking, they won't start.

- Unsolicited agenda items proposed by the rest of the room. I'm not talking about the ones you ask for, I'm talking about the agenda items that just appear. These random new additions are emerging proof that the rest of the room is beginning to see that this is a meeting where work is done. It's another positive health sign.

Staff meetings are an hour. It feels like a lot of time, but when this meeting is working you'll effortlessly fill the time.

It's a rolling agenda because the steady healthy state for this meeting is that you never get through the agenda—there are too many topics to discuss.

Gossip, Rumors, and Lies is the final permanent agenda item. In the last 5 to 10 minutes of your meeting, you need to carve out some time for communication error correction. I'll explain.

The reason you're having this meeting is because of a seismic shift. Your team suddenly grew, your company changed direction, major responsibilities shifted, or maybe a reorganization occurred. The knee-jerk move when a shift takes place is to call all the relevant parties into the room and ask, "WTF?" This feels good. People talk and explain their feelings about the change. Information is shared, and we all nod and feel aligned—but while the therapy is nice, we didn't solve whatever problem existed that precipitated the need for this meeting. Meetings are a symptom of a disease, not the cure.

The metrics framing and rolling agenda should give you an actionable narrative. They should provide the opportunity for the airing and discussion of grievances. They should create a set of follow-up work that is far more likely the cure. However, you should still be asking, "WTF?"

This final section of your staff meeting is a safe place for all participants to raise any issues, to ask any random questions, or to confirm any hallway or Slack chatter. Chances are, whatever seismic event caused this meeting to occur is still being organizationally digested, and often the stories being told are absurd. Gossip, Rumors, and Lies is time to get that important absurdity out in the open, so you can begin to construct a healthy response.

Meetings Are a Symptom, Not the Cure

High on my list of professional pet peeves is the emergence of corrosive politics within a company. Politics are a natural development in a large group of humans working together. Corrosive politics give me rage. Taking credit for others' ideas, hoarding information, not allowing the best idea to win—the list goes on and on, and when I discover this type of politics where I work there is rage. So, I've spent a good portion of my career seeking to understand the root causes.

Seismic shifts within a company or team create change, and humans attempting to get work done consistently while maintaining velocity and high standards don't like change. It harshes their productivity buzz. The intensity of their response to change is a function of their discomfort, and that discomfort increases exponentially the longer its source remains unresolved.

The reason meetings have evolved as an acceptable first response is because they address one key issue: they give the team an opportunity to discuss their perceptions of the change. This feels *good*. The reason meetings are often hated is because while talking feels good, it's not true progress.

If you've called the meeting for the right reason, if you've discovered story-filled metrics, if you build a compelling team-sourced agenda, if you give everyone time to discuss the absurd, and if you share the insights from this meeting with the whole company, you've given the team a chance to collectively resolve the core issue. The sharing of this work will decrease miscommunication, help inoculate against politics, and create unexpected serendipity.

No one is going to just sit there when they understand the problems at hand, they trust they can be heard, and they can count on resolution.

14

Rainbows and Unicorns

Peggle is a casual game developed by PopCap. Originally released in 2007, the game is memorable because of its absolutely over-the-top level-finishing sequence (*https://youtu.be/wWMPDvUh2YI*).

In an explosion of rainbows, fireworks, unicorns, and Beethoven's "Ode to Joy," you are generously and emotionally rewarded when you finish a level. As a friend commented, "It is likely the most consistent and unadulterated source of positive feedback you'll get in your life."

The gaming industry has spent billions of dollars successfully figuring out how to design and build products that provide Peggle moments—that tap into the parts of your brain that reward specific behavior. Game developers know when to reward you in order to keep you entertained and engaged. Some products and companies do this well, and others are total douchebags about how they choose to reinforce behavior. Regardless, the rules are tried and true and deeply wired into your brain.

And there is absolutely no way they can't be used for good (or evil) in any product, team, or company.

Moments of Disproportionate Satisfaction

I've been thinking about games for a long time, and I believe there are three rules that define a good game:

- I have a continual, healthy sense of progression.
- I am learning and mastering the game via timely and effective feedback.
- I have the impression that I can win.

True story: I wrote versions of this chapter for a good two years. The vastness of the gaming domain paralyzed me each time I attempted to finish. But as I've edited, I've realized that these rules also apply to building a healthy team. In particular, the second one: *I am learning and mastering the game—the system—via timely and effective feedback.*

What a horribly dry rule. I need to spice up my wisdom with a dose of poetry, so how about a more specific version: "compliments work."

Duh

I'll write about the two other rules and how they relate to good leadership and a healthy team another time. This chapter is about the power of a compliment. A compliment is *a selfless, well-articulated, and timely recognition of achievement.* To start to understand the value of a compliment, let's go back to that Peggle video. Play it again.

It's a visual and auditory feast full of familiar sights and sounds designed to give you joy.

When it comes to the motivation of humans, we've designed all sorts of communications tools and interesting cultural artifacts to help us move forward. Here's a deadline that clearly tells us when we should be done. Here's a Gantt chart to explain where we are as a team and how we collectively get from here to there. I am assertive, which means folks who like to be told what to do will appreciate my communication style. All of these structures, articles, ways of communicating, and threats can motivate, but game makers have learned the elegant motivational properties of a compliment. Allow me to demonstrate:

> *Thank you for reading this book. I spent hours on these articles. I fret over them, I love them, and then I hate them. Eventually, I toss them into the world wondering what you'll think. If you're still here, I don't know if you liked this piece or not, but I do know that you've spent just under five minutes of your life reading something I wrote, which means I held your interest, so thank you. I appreciate every single one of my readers.*

Are you feeling it? You should, because I mean it.

Peggle rewards you when you perform a simple task. It's saccharine and over the top, but you can't say that Peggle doesn't own the compliment. The game's developers want you to celebrate your achievement in the loudest, most ludicrous way, and it works.

However, the Peggle compliment does fail to meet my definition. While it is a timely and well-articulated recognition of achievement, it is hardly selfless. It's fun, but it's designed to be fun so that you keep playing the game. It's a timely endorphin boost that is designed to train your brain to crave finishing because... that head-banging unicorn (*https://oreil.ly/oWIQH*). He's the *best*.

Let's decompose a useful compliment.

The Compliment Breakdown

Once more, my definition of a compliment: a selfless, well-articulated, and timely recognition of achievement. Let's take that apart.

First up, the reason this compliment needs to exist is the *achievement*. This human did something notable, and you want to recognize this fact. The magnitude of achievement is a factor, but I find compliments small and large carry the same weight. You want to highlight when the team or team members are at their best; you want to recognize meaningful acts of being human.

Recognition is what you're trying to provide, but how do you go about this? Is this a compliment you want to land 1:1 at the moment the achievement occurs, or is it the type of compliment that you want to tuck away so you can land it in front of the entire team for maximum recognition? I don't know. There are so many contextual variables to consider here that it's hard to give universal advice. Do they need to hear it? Or do others need to hear it about them? Understand what behavior you want to recognize, and why, and make a call.

Timeliness is the easiest attribute to understand. My default is to compliment as quickly as possible because I believe it's the most effective way to reinforce behavior. That's what we're doing here, right? The blandest version of what you're saying is, "This thing you do is important." The less time you take to make the compliment, the more they're going to remember—not the compliment itself, but the act that led to the compliment.

Well-articulated is the attribute that is the hardest to define and the most important. Let's start with what looks like a horrible compliment. The vapid "Good job!" seems like an F, right? Not true. A well-timed "Good job!" can be an effective and timely recognition of achievement. Even better, how about this?

Thank you for taking the time to build the technical overview document for Q&A. The feature you built is great, and now we better understand not only how to test it, but how to support it.

This compliment specifically documents the act, the value, and the impact. It is that detailed articulation that will make it most memorable.

The most nuanced part of a compliment is *selflessness*. This is also entirely context-dependent, but a good compliment is one that comes without perceived social cost or dependency. You know what doghouse roses are? They're flowers you buy for your significant other because you screwed up. Yes, they are pretty, but all the recipient sees in those roses is your screw-up. It's a thoughtless, empty gift that erodes trust. A good compliment contains nothing about you or what you want. It is entirely about the achievement of the other human.

A Compliment Career Shift

What are the moments that defined your career? Sure, I bet you can rattle off the disasters, because the mental blast radius of a disaster has staying power. Keep thinking. I suspect you can think of a few compliments that changed the course of your career.

At my first start-up, a senior VP of engineering who ran brusque and terse was working with me on compensation adjustments for the team. We were efficiently and quietly working our way through a spreadsheet and comparing notes. Halfway through the spreadsheet, he looked up at me and out of nowhere said the longest sentence of the day, "Understanding people is your superpower, Lopp. Don't forget that."

A well-constructed compliment has an emotional payload. It is full of rainbows and unicorns. It's this strange, unpredictable payload that makes us nervous about compliments. But when made selflessly and used for good, a compliment is an elegant and lasting way to recognize and reward when people are showcasing the best versions of themselves.

Say the Hard Thing

On my short list of critical leadership skills, the ability to "say the hard thing" is right after "delegate until it hurts." The majority of people-related disasters I've created have originated with my choice to not say the hard thing.

I didn't give feedback when behavior was off because the person was new and I told myself, "Give them time to adjust. They're new." A month later the unchecked behavior had grown (because I hadn't said anything), but I didn't give feedback again because, ya know, in a month we're doing formal feedback so I'll just give it then, right?

The difficulty with saying the hard thing is you know how it will feel to hear the hard thing. You're projecting yourself into the mind of the receiver and literally feeling their reaction. Thank you for being an empathic leader. However, your job, the work you should value the most, is helping your team grow. Compliments and recognition are one way to highlight exceptional work, but saying the hard thing always gets their attention.

The Voice in Your Head

There's a constant voice in your head. That voice is saying each of the words you read here right now. You have mapped this voice to what you consider the Rands voice to be, but it's not my voice. It is what you want the Rands voice to sound like, and it's entirely your creation.

Hi. You're awesome.

This voice works in your favor. It translates everything you experience into digestible constructs that you can understand, and it often biases these constructs toward your hopes and dreams. It is optimistic. This is *well researched* (*https://oreil.ly/Oo3bK*) and normal. We are all the heroes of our own story. This voice tells the story of the world from your perspective, passed through the sum total of your experiences, translated into information, morphed into judgment, and often resulting in the creation of incremental wisdom.

This voice is also often wrong or just misinformed, especially when you fail.

You're embarrassed or ashamed when you fail. Maybe you're mad, but after the initial emotion churn passes, you protectively rationalize. You find a narrative about the failure that is acceptable in the context of *what you currently know*. What did you learn? How will you proceed? What story will you tell others about this failure? All of this is defined by how you process your failure.

Notice a pattern here? You are missing critical data when all you consult is yourself. It's not that your inner dialog has a devious plan to prevent you from learning, it's that it's operating with an incomplete and biased set of data. The humans around you, watching you act, have the additional context and the experience required to make important observations about both your successes and your failures.

How does this relate back to saying the hard thing? When we don't want to say the hard thing we exacerbate the problem because we have the same voice in our head telling us, "It would be hard for me to hear this, so I don't want to say it." Worse, in the manager/employee relationship, the historic professional incentives are designed to prevent us from saying the hard thing. Your voice cautiously advises you, "They write your review. They set your compensation. You cannot tell them that. They'll be mad."

Let's fix this. There are two practices: learning to say the hard thing followed by actively hearing the hard thing.

Saying the Hard Thing

A good place to start practicing feedback is with new employees. Once we're past the "getting to know you" phase of a working relationship, a month or two in, I start giving feedback. I keep it lightweight at first ("In this meeting, you said this thing. Is this what you meant to say?"), and at the end of each 1:1 I ask the same question, "Do you have any feedback for me?"

They never do. That's okay. It can take months. It took a former CEO a year before they took me up on my incessant feedback requests. Feedback is about building trust, and we humans are extremely slow to trust. It's cool. Take your time. I am patient because I understand what is at stake: the health of our working relationship.

In each 1:1, I keep providing feedback ("During that presentation for your team, you were acting this way. Is this what you were meaning to portray?").

Same drill as before; I then ask, "Do you have any feedback for me?" Finally, weeks after I first give them the opportunity, they realize I'm not going to stop asking—so they give me some feedback, and it's a test because they want to see how I am going to react.

"You weren't prepared for that all hands."

I wasn't.

Hearing the Hard Thing

The first time someone gives you critical feedback, it's a test for everyone involved. The giver is taking a risk because you're the boss and they've seen prior bosses lose their s—t when they've received feedback. Now, hopefully for well-intentioned reasons, they are giving you—the receiver—this gift, with the hope that it is useful.[1]

There are three classes of feedback:

- *No big deal* feedback is no big deal. You hear it, you accept it, you update your priors, and you move along with your slightly altered worldview. Your goal in life is to make all feedback in all directions no big deal. This is hard.

- *Slow burn* feedback feels like No Big Deal until you're driving home from work and realize there was unexpected depth to the feedback. There was critical feedback in what felt easy to understand, and with time you realize it's...

- *Just plain hard* feedback is different. In many cases, I can tell when hard feedback is about to arrive. There could be a sudden change in the tone of the conversation; it might be a one-off meeting that doesn't normally happen; or I might simply notice a strange new expression. Whatever the leading indicator, my brain quickly predicts a complex moment arriving and moves into high alert mode. *I am literally preparing for hand-to-hand combat in my head.*

Hard feedback, critical feedback, is distilled truth.[2] In the days and weeks full of vapid "How ya doings?" "Great jobs," and high fives, hard feedback represents

---

1 It always is. Even if it's misinformed or outright untrue, it's useful.

2 Okay, sometimes it's a complete lie, but the fact that this person is choosing to tell you this lie is interesting information all by itself.

a rarely seen report on the state of your ability. When the feedback is hard, there is another two-step process for making sure you don't miss anything.

Step 1: *No matter how critical the feedback, listen and search for just a glimpse of understanding.* Why only a glimpse? I'm glad you asked.

Remember: Brain. High alert. You're going to instinctively want to respond, to react, to do something to protect yourself from the *fight*—but at this point, you don't actually know how to react. You haven't unpacked the feedback, so most reactions are emotional and pointless. You must listen to each word and seek a neutral understanding, even with the hard feedback pointed directly at your face.

I was unprepared for the all hands? DO YOU KNOW HOW MUCH TIME I SPENT ON THAT DECK? I HAVEN'T SLEPT IN TWO NIGHTS BECAUSE I WAS SO NERVOUS, AND BY THE WAY...

The yelling is your brain defending its poorly informed reality, but the yelling distracts you from hearing anything. It has taken years to train myself, but now the moment I hear the beginning of hard feedback, I adopt the position: crossed legs, folded hands, head slightly tilted. This is my "I am listening" position. It reminds me to listen.

Listen for what? One simple insight. One realization. Here's one example: "Why are they choosing to give me this feedback right now?" The trick is to engage your rational brain, the part of your brain that likes to solve problems, as opposed to the part that wants to scream, because the part of your brain that wants to scream is exceptional at demonstrating tremendously poor judgment.

Sometimes the feedback shocks you so much that understanding is impossible—which leads us to our second step.

Step 2: *Repeat what you heard.*

You will be shocked by the usefulness of this simple advice. Even if you achieve the pure listening zen prescribed in step 1, you are still building your own version of the narrative. And when the feedback is shocking, your narrative is going to be somewhere between slightly and completely wrong. So, repeat what you heard. This both clarifies and acknowledges the feedback:

ME: *"Just so I'm clear what you're saying, you're saying that I didn't perform well at the all hands?"*

THEM: *"No, I didn't say that. You're a delight to watch speak, but you weren't prepared. The narrative didn't hold up and I think you think being eloquent is making up for the fact that your thesis wasn't sound."*

ME: *Oh.*

Your Goal in Life

Again, your goal in life is to make feedback in all directions no big deal. You and your team never start in this state; you work up to it. You start with small spoken observations that slowly turn into more useful feedback. You watch each other to see if you're listening to the feedback, and eventually acting on it.[3] Once everyone has seen that feedback is both shared and acted on, you begin to feel more comfortable sharing larger, more complex, and harder feedback. Why? Trust.

Feedback is an incredibly valuable social transaction. It shows that people have taken their time to observe an aspect of you. They have other things to do, but today they are investing in you. You think you've got it all figured out, but you don't. In turn, you take the time to clearly hear the feedback, ask clarifying questions, and hopefully adjust the way you work.

All the constituent parts of the act of giving and receiving feedback provide an opportunity to build trust in a relationship.

---

3 I've left the hardest part of this practice out: processing and, if appropriate, acting on the feedback in a timely fashion. Take a look at Chapters 7 and 28 for ideas on how to start work here.

16

Everything Breaks

We're going to play a really simple, really dumb game. I'll explain the setup and the rules:

- Choose two one-person "teams."
- On a flat, boring surface, draw two parallel 3-foot-long white lines that are 50 feet apart.
- Each team chooses a home base line. The other line marks the opposing team's home base.
- The teams start by standing completely behind their home base lines while facing the opposing team.

The goal of this game is to earn points. A point is earned when a player's entire body crosses their home line, then the opposing line, and finally their home line again. The first team to 20 points wins.

Like I said, simple and dumb.

You already have questions. *Can I interfere with the other player? Who is judging and counting the points? What do I win?* Good questions, but I'd argue that with the rule set above you have a minimally viable game. You can start to play the game with little fuss. It's going to be furious (and lame) sprinting back and forth, but you can play.

Third Time's a Charm

I'm working on my third rapid-growth start-up in a row. This phase in a company's growth is my jam: the enthusiasm, the ambition, the plethora of blank slates. Very little is defined. Even less is written down. Everyone is fired up. *We're going to figure this out as we go...thank you very much.*

Over the past decade I've written *hundreds of pieces (https://oreil.ly/LIPSh),* some based on company-specific observations and others on eerie patterns that keep appearing amongst companies with vastly different cultures, products, and businesses. One such pattern is the Rule of 3 and 10 (*https://oreil.ly/drFz6*). As told by a former Evernote CEO:

> When you go from one person to three people it's different. When it's just you, you know what you are doing and then you have three people and you have to rethink how you are doing everything. But when there are 10 people it's all going to change again. And when there are 30 people it will change again. Same when you reach a hundred people.
>
> At every one of those steps everything kind of breaks. Everything. Your communication systems and your payroll and your accounting and customer support. Everything that you put into place needs to change when you put in those 3 and 10 steps.

I can confidently confirm based on my experience that things fall apart as a function of the number of humans involved, with eerie predictability. But how? And why?

Game On

Thought experiment. Add 18 people to the game: 9 on each side, totaling 10 per team. More importantly, don't tell any of them the rules beforehand. Upon their arrival, it's on you, the newly anointed team captain, to explain the rules, make sure everyone understands them, and ensure the game is played cleanly and fairly. However, you have just *two minutes* from start to finish to explain the game before the starting gun fires.

Okay? Ready. Go.

You don't have to actually play the game to understand that the 10-versus-10-person version of the Simple Dumb Game is going to be a s—t show. Remember, our starting white line suggests a heretofore unspecified queuing system for our 10-person teams. The basic rules are woefully incomplete on the topic of multi-person starts. Interference, a curiosity with solo-player teams, is a nightmare with 20. Finally, you have our two respective teams, who are looking at their respective captains who took two whole minutes to explain the rules. The teams wonder, "Why are we playing this stupid game?"

In the one-on-one version of the game, it's a simple foot race. Run back and forth, cross the line. Maybe...*maybe* one of the players realizes that interference is not mentioned in the rules and is perhaps legal (*It is. Also, no referees. Bonus!*), so they attempt to slow the other player down as they cross paths. Chances are, it's just a crazy amount of running hither and fro with the winner being the faster runner.

In the 10-versus-10 version, it's a disaster. Even the best coach will be challenged by relaying even the simple rules to nine other humans in two minutes. With the woefully incomplete set of rules in hand, the game starts okay. One player goes at a time, until someone figures out there is no rule governing the number of players that can be on the field and there's a rush of players from one side. Then the other team sees the rush and does the same.

Now they're getting creative. If a team is behind, why not block the opposing team from crossing their narrow three-foot line? (*Allowed.*) Why not send players multiple times to get more points on the board? (*Also allowed.*) Let's be clear, the Simple Dumb Game wasn't remotely fun at one versus one, but now it's utter chaos. A poorly defined and poorly communicated rule set *which has not even been tested with humans at 10-versus-10 scale* has created mayhem.

And this is just a simple, dumb game. What about the rules governing your company? Sure, no one calls them "rules," but buried within your company culture is a set of complex and fascinating operating principles. Some are spoken. Many are not. Everyone must discover them, and 10 new humans are starting at your company next Monday. With their arrival, what is going to break for the first time?

With Alarming Predictability

The Stupid Dumb Game teaches us three principles:

1. Humans will greatly benefit from a clear explanation of the rules of the game.

2. The rules need to evolve in unexpected ways to account for the arrival of more humans.

3. The only way to effectively learn what is going to break is to keeping playing...and learning.

These principles frame my advice for your growing company:

1. Provide a clear explanation of the rules.

2. Be prepared for the rules to evolve in unexpected ways.

3. Play, learn, and repeat.

PROVIDE A CLEAR EXPLANATION OF THE RULES

The goal of your onboarding program is to get the new humans up to speed and productive as quickly as possible. Each of my past three start-ups has invested in onboarding programs, with the most recent being the most thoughtful. At each start-up, we should have invested five times as much.

The challenge with investing in onboarding, as with most investments in the humans at your company, is proving a compelling and measurable return on that investment. Everyone agrees that onboarding feels like a thing we should invest in, but isn't the first priority building and selling a product?

It was. It's not now. When it was two of you working in the garage, no one cared about onboarding because sans a product there is nothing actually to board. However, you are now a legion of humans, and the product you are building is a business.

Your onboarding program has three sections. Yes, everyone also has questions regarding health benefits and when they get paid, but those answers are quick and straightforward. The topics of substance you must describe are:

Our vision

What is the ambitious mountain we are climbing? Why are we doing it? And what is going to happen when we get there?

Our values

On this journey, how do we want to treat ourselves and others? Why did we pick these values? What do these values teach us? What do they look like in practice?

Our practices

What are the specific proven practices we use on this journey to get things done? How do we build together?[1]

---

1 For as long as possible, the humans who are building the company with their hands need to be regularly featured speakers in your onboarding programs.

The content of each section varies wildly by business and by the population of humans. Chances are, even if you haven't written down the content, it's 80% defined in an amorphous spoken-word existing-in-the-hallway fashion. Chances are, the new humans walking in the door are assuming this work is 100% done and 100% available, because they want to know the rules of the game as quickly as possible.

ALLOW THE RULES TO EVOLVE IN UNEXPECTED WAYS

At a start-up, "fail fast" isn't good advice; it's a way of life, and it's the defining characteristic. It is up to you to make failure a competitive advantage.

Failure is an opportunity to learn. Yes, you should put out the failure fire as quickly as possible, but the moment the fire is out you need to begin a systematic, efficient, and familiar process of figuring out how it started so you can prevent it from happening again.

The first start-up I worked at after Apple was particularly good at this. We used a Five Whys (*https://oreil.ly/EZjWZ*) type of process not just when there was a significant failure in the product, but when there was a substantial failure in any part of the business. Why didn't this key hire accept? Investigate. Why are new hires not getting their offer letters? Dig in. We took the time to understand each failure deeply and to find the root cause so we could begin to build a proper fix.

The identification of the critical fixes resulting from the failures you experience represents one of your best defenses against future failures—but you need to finish.

PLAY, LEARN, AND REPEAT

Here's the deal. Your company probably already does onboarding. You probably know the name of the human in the building who bangs the table preaching about postmortem processes. Disasters have occurred, and someone ran to the internet for help. They read an article just like this years ago, discovered a compelling argument for onboarding or postmortems, assigned a DRI[2] to the task, and moved on to the next crisis. My question: did they fix the problem?

My third and last piece of advice is the hardest. When things break, you must *learn from the failure.*

---

2 Directly responsible individual.

I was feeling pretty good about our postmortem process at a prior start-up. It was engineering-focused (not company-wide), but we trained folks in running an efficient postmortem, we took copious notes, and we religiously logged next actions in our bug tracking system.

After a particularly bad incident, I read the postmortem write-up, and something seemed familiar. A quick scan of the bug database revealed we'd triggered the same bug that had been discovered during a prior incident. A critical bug logged, but not fixed. Becoming alarmed, I ran the following query: "How many issues identified by a postmortem have been resolved as fixed?"

14%.

In our fury to fix, we forgot to finish.

An epic failure has the unique attribute that when it occurs, you have everyone's attention. It is relatively easy to instigate change after an epic failure because everyone is staring at the sky, not blinking, prepared for it to fall once more. Learning from epic failures isn't hard. Disciplined learning from all failures requires thoughtful work.

I can't think of a better inoculation to what ails all rapidly growing companies than building a healthy culture of learning from failure—which means not just identifying the critical fixes, but acting on them. Completely implementing them. You're thinking I'm talking about bugs in your product, but I am also talking about critical bugs in your company.

Failure as a Competitive Differentiator (Or, Don't Play Dumb Games Twice)

The timing, type, and severity of failures at scale vary by company, team...and culture. With alarming predictability, at specific team sizes, these failures cluster. The humans see the spike in failures, become alarmed, start worrying to each other, and create a fear feedback loop. This is going to occur no matter what. It's a cost of running a growing business.

What is this fear based on? Depends on the failure, but it's likely a combination of:

- Did leadership see this coming? (*Nope.*)

- If they did, why didn't they prevent it from happening? (*Didn't see it coming. Couldn't prevent it.*)

- I saw this coming, I raised my hand, and no one did anything. (*I wish we'd listened. I'm sorry.*)

- Is it going to happen again? (*Not like this, if I have anything to say about it.*)
- Who is in trouble? (*No one.*)

One of my favorite worry-in-the-middle-of-the-night threads is trying to predict what is going to break before it's broken—wasted calories. Everything breaks. Failure is created by the increasing entropy of a growing number of humans running around the building, good intentions in hand, breaking things.

Once they're broken, and with ruthless and calming efficiency, you must set to the task of learning. What truly broke here? What is the best set of fixes? Who is accountable for leading those fixes? It won't completely address the fear, but a culture of learning and acting on those learnings will signal to everyone that you take failure seriously and are eager to learn completely.

Okay? Ready. Go.

17

The Org Chart Test

If you've had a 1:1 with me in the last decade, you know that once we're done with our planned agenda there's a good chance that I'll stand up, walk to the whiteboard, and start drawing some version of the organization chart (*org chart*).

I believe the org chart is a critical artifact that must be easily discoverable and well maintained. Why? Let's start with a definition. In my favorite part of my first book, *Managing Humans*—the glossary—I define an org chart as:

> *A visual representation of who reports to whom. Org charts are handy in large organizations for figuring out who you're dealing with.*

That's one good use case, but there's one missing. An org chart should also effectively describe, at a high level, how the product is organized and who is responsible for what. Above all, an org chart should be legible.

The Legibility Test

Grab a coworker (doesn't matter who), head to the nearest empty conference room with a whiteboard, grab a colored pen and make sure it's not a Sharpie™, and start scribbling. We're looking for an org chart.

Rands, how should I draw it? Boxes and arrows? Architecture? People structure? Technical structure? Which boxes go where? I need guidance.

For this exercise, the only guidance I'll provide is no names of human beings.[1] Please draw what you consider to be the most commonly understood version of the org chart.

---

1 When proper names show up on an org chart, it transforms into a different beast. It's an equally important artifact, but when names land on the org chart, it becomes less organizational and more political.

Done? Okay. Here are a series of increasingly complex questions your drawing should answer.

First, *did you draw something useful?* Seems like a simple part of the task, right? I do candidate interviews all the time, so I've got this drawing down, but I wonder about you. How quickly can you step up, draw some boxes, and give them names? Are you happy with the result?

Next, ask yourself: *At any point during the drawing process, did you stop to explain yourself? Are there parts where you're making excuses for the way it's drawn?* As you were drawing the boxes, did you need to stop and say, "Yeah, this is weird, but..." or "You probably think this box means *this*, but it means *that*"? If, like me, you've drawn this picture a lot, you probably don't even hear yourself making these excuses because that's *just the way you've always described it.*

When you're a small team—say, less than one hundred—the org chart isn't that important because the humans can keep the state of the team in their heads. Nothing needs to be written down because communication is freely flowing. The communication tax of large organizations has not yet been applied. The humans know who is responsible for what. They know who owns different parts of the stack. They must. It's a small company, and the ownership of things is changing all the time because...it's a start-up. Chaos is the defining characteristic.

But at some point, someone on the team is talking to an interview candidate, and they realize they need to draw a visual representation of the team. It's crude. It's fast. And it's the very first org chart. More on this in a moment, but first back to the test.

Final question. *If you left the org chart on the whiteboard[2] and a random tenured human on the team walked by the conference room and saw it, would they nod and say, "Yup, that's about right"?* The tax on communication increases as a function of the size of the team. The reason you need agreed-upon and well-understood artifacts like an org chart is because they make critical aspects of the organization clear. Everyone then understands the critical truths.

This final question is impossible to answer objectively. You need to answer the question subjectively: Is my org chart legible? Is it clear enough to read? Could your average employee, without any outside help, read your org chart and answer the following questions?

---

2 Don't do this. It freaks people out. See above.

- What are the constituent parts of the team?

- It is clear from the names of the different teams who is likely responsible for what within the team?

- Does how the org chart is drawn give the reader a high-level idea of how the product or business is architected?

Management types take this artifact for granted because we live it. Our day is full of travels across the org chart. It's our mental map for the humans and technologies within our teams, which means we both understand it and take it for granted. The vast majority of the humans in your organization do not have a daily need to comprehend the org chart, but when they do, your goal is instant maximum legibility.

The Basics at Scale

How much time does your team spend thinking about obvious things? It's a tricky question for a manager to answer, because the job gives you extraordinary access to information. There are daily reminders of the obvious.

But the communication tax applied to large teams ensures that the basic information doesn't scale without structured assistance. The org chart, the company values, and the current business goals: this critical information must become a set of easily discoverable and well-maintained artifacts. When the humans have a question, your goal is that they habitually return to these artifacts to answer their obvious questions because they are full of critical truths.

Back to our rapidly growing start-up. There's a critical inflection point when someone somewhere in the building thinks, "We need managers" and 12.3 seconds later they draw a people-based org chart on the nearest piece of paper. *Jules can work with these folks. Kate can manage these humans. Okay. Whew. Next crisis.*

This is backwards. Jules and Kate are lovely humans and perfectly capable of being managers, but building an org chart around the humans is the wrong approach. What are you building? An ecommerce site? Rad. You likely have a frontend team and a backend team. Build your first org chart around your product or the technology, not the people.

A people-based org chart describes power structures. Who is responsible for whom? What do they own? How big is their area of influence? Whom do they report to? You cannot avoid these questions being asked, but you can set the tone for how you view your organizational structures. Product first? Technology first? Or people first?

I share this advice with you because it's a mistake I made for years. Initial conditions set a tone that is nigh impossible to change.

18

A Distributed Meeting Primer

As a leader who primarily values team health, I place great store in the weekly 1:1 because it's where I assess the health of my team members. It's my highest-bandwidth meeting. Some of those meetings are held via videoconference with humans around the world. For years, there was a slight to significant lag omnipresent in these discussions that stilted the conversation. The lag was a persistent reminder of the distance between me and my teammates.

Combined with the incredibly predictable audio/video gymnastics that accompanied the start of these meetings, this impediment often led to the same frustrated thought: "There has got to be a better way."

For the past three years or so, my perception has been that videoconferencing is a solved problem. The combination of mature networking infrastructure and well-designed software has mostly eliminated the lag and significantly decreased the A/V gymnastics.

Nevertheless, we still have work to do.

Remote

Let's start with the word *remote*. Remote team. Remote worker. The word means "situated far from the main centers of the population," which in the context of the workplace is usually factually inaccurate—a remote team or human is simply one that is not at headquarters. But it's what most people think of when they say "remote," and that's the first problem.

Let's start by agreeing on two ideas:

- Call these remote humans and teams *distributed* instead. Distributed is a boring word, but it is in that boringness that we solve one issue. *Remote* implies *far from the center*, whereas *distributed* means *elsewhere*.

- Agree that no matter what we call them, humans and teams that are elsewhere are at a professional disadvantage.[1] There is a communication, culture, and context tax applied to folks who are distributed.[2] Your job as a leader is to actively invest in reducing that tax.

Good? Let's start with something simple: a brief list of tactical advice about the mechanics of running a distributed meeting.

The "Many People" Meeting

The use case I'm going to talk about is a complex and wasteful one. Much of the following prescriptive tactical advice applies to the 1:1 meetings you'll have with distributed team members too, but let's focus where there is the most pain, the most cost, and the most room for improvement: the "many people" meeting.

In the many people meeting, you have two locations: *host* and *distributed*. Host is where the majority of the humans are located, and distributed is where we find the humans on the various other ends of a videoconference call.

I've already written about *the rules* (*https://oreil.ly/qkL1c*) for this type of meeting. I'd suggest reading that article and considering the following challenge: how do we make this meeting the same experience for all parties, so as to create the same amount of value for everyone?

My advice for leaders who regularly conduct distributed meetings falls into three categories: Pre-Meeting, During, and Post-Meeting.

---

1 Disclaimer: this discussion is based on a distributed team scenario where there is a headquarters—a base of operations that contains a good chunk of the humans. There is a variant where everyone in the company is distributed around the world. That is super interesting, but I've never experienced it. There's a chance that the advice in this chapter is useful in an all-distributed scenario too, but buyer beware.

2 And there are distinct advantages, too.

PRE-MEETING

- Don't chintz on audio/video hardware and networking.[3]

- Schedule meetings at X:05 or X:35 and get there at X:00 to make sure all the technology is set up for a distributed meeting. Not only does this ensure the meeting starts on time, but it sends an important signal. How often have you had a meeting where, seven minutes in, someone asks, "Where's Andy?" Well, Andy is distributed, and no one on the host side turned on the video camera. More importantly, Andy has been sitting in his home office for the last seven minutes wondering, "Did they forget me?"

- Set sensible defaults in your audio/videoconferencing software. Default your microphone and audio to "off" when you enter a new meeting. This reduces the interruption factor when you join the meeting.

- Check your background. Anything distracting behind you? Fix it.

- Is the whiteboard in play? Great. Make sure it's readable to distributed folks before the meeting.

DURING

- Assign a spotter on the host side. This is the human responsible for paying attention to the distributed folks and looking for visual cues that they are ready to speak.

- Understand the acoustic attributes of a room. Is this the first time this particular set of humans are meeting in a distributed fashion? Do a microphone check for everyone right at the start. If there is horrible background noise on the distributed side, headphones are helpful.

- Encourage participants to hit mute if they are not speaking. Microphones often capture more sound than you expect. Especially typing. Wait, who's typing? Follow the same protocol as if everyone were in the same room: no laptops except for the note taker.

---

3 Think about how much you're paying the team, and then think about how much it costs you to have them inefficiently communicate with each other on crappy infrastructure.

- When focus shifts to the whiteboard, confirm (again) that distributed folks can see the whiteboard. Another excellent job for the spotter.

- The room with the most people disconnects last. Respect.

POST-MEETING

- For a first-time meeting with these humans or in this space, ask how it went for everyone. Fix things that are broken.

- You may learn that some distributed folks couldn't hear well during the meeting. Invest in fixing bad audio in conference rooms. Especially in large host rooms, multiple microphones can capture the strangest set of sounds. At a prior gig, the boardroom had microphones built into the table. One exec liked to click their pen during the meeting, under the table. For distributed folks, it was a deafening CLICK CLICK CLICK that the folks in the host room couldn't even hear.

- Given the likelihood that the distributed folks missed something during the meeting—which is a thing to be fixed—the distribution of the meeting notes provides a critical feedback loop for everyone who took part. The value of these notes decays rapidly, so send them as quickly as possible.

No Measurable Difference

Much of the leadership work I've done around distributed teams centers not on resolving concerns about how the audio/visual equipment works in a meeting, but on how a distributed team feels treated by headquarters. It's never just one thing: it's a long list of grievances that combine into the erroneous but very real perception that a distributed team is somehow less important.

Much of the advice I've given here is tactical—simple acts to facilitate better communication—but in combination it supports a broader goal. By making sure every human in the meeting has equal access to the communication and the context, we send a clear message that being distributed doesn't matter. There is no measurable difference if you are in the host room or distributed.

Slack: Executive

THE STORY AS I HEARD IT WAS Stewart Butterfield likes games and has twice attempted to build a commercially viable online game. The first one was called Game Neverending. Built during the first generation of the internet, it was not a success. But one aspect of the game appeared valuable: sharing photos.

The company that built Game Neverending, Ludicorp, pivoted and built Flickr for the world. Butterfield sold Flickr (at 40 people) to Yahoo! and remained there as the GM for four years. Upon leaving Yahoo! he made his second game attempt with Glitch, with his company Tiny Speck. Web-based, artistically delicious, and weirdly clever, Glitch didn't find a viable market. As Butterfield attempted to return investors' money, they asked, "Do you have any other ideas?"

He did.

In building Glitch, the team had hacked on a version of Internet Relay Chat (IRC) to make it more useful for team collaboration. They could not imagine building anything else without this janky communication tool, so they chose to build the janky communication tool from the ground up—and that changed everything.

Pivoting and rebranding the company, they built a beta in six months. They signed up 8,000 companies in 24 hours and quickly discovered they'd built the fastest-growing piece of enterprise software in the history of the galaxy. They called it Slack.

I was in love with Slack long before Stewart mailed me. It was not that I was a longtime IRC user—it was just obvious to me that communication among teams must evolve. It could be much faster to find, contact, and communicate with another human. There would be less time lost endlessly managing an inbox. We would finally build a living repository of knowledge. Problem was, I loved my current job.

Stewart wrote, "And Michael, what harm could it possibly do to talk?"
What possible harm indeed...

My title when I was hired at Slack was Vice President of Engineering. My prior role at Pinterest was Head of Engineering. Titles, as we learned in the introduction to Act II, vary by the culture, but the responsibilities are the same. Unlike at Pinterest, at Slack I shared senior engineering leadership responsibilities with cofounder and CTO Cal Henderson.

I was in an executive role at Pinterest for almost two years. Slack probably thought I was an "experienced executive leader." As it turned out, two of those words were correct. The first and the last.

It takes three years—minimum—to become competent at a new job. *Three years minimum.* This meant that when I arrived at Slack I was still 12 months from truly understanding and being competent at the role of executive.

Why am I telling you this at the beginning of the third act? Two reasons. First, you already knew leadership was hard, so why make it harder right out of the gate? Second, you won't believe me anyway until you've seen with your own eyeballs how long it takes to become proficient at a complex job.

The sense of distance that started when you became a manager of managers is truly impressive as an executive. You are now responsible for an entire business or organization, which means not only are you far from the work, but you're far from the teams as well. Oh yeah—and you're accountable for all of it.

This responsibility is accompanied by the toughest aspect of the executive role, which is that fires burn faster uphill. When something catches fire on one team, there is a manager there who hopefully competently handles the fire. Sometimes they can't. The fire gains strength and speed, and it's escalated to their director, who with their additional experience can often put out the now significant blaze. Sometimes they can't. Sometimes the magnitude of the disaster is beyond the ability of your whole team, so they escalate it to you.

As an executive, the majority of unexpected situations you'll face are prequalified five-alarm fires. They are the worst possible version of the situation. And that's just Monday.

Strange, right? So, what do executives do all day? Fight fires? Yes, but our primary job is fire *prevention*. What combination of people, products, and processes is necessary to build the highest-quality product? Figuring that out is the easy part of the executive's job. Here's the hard part: what combination of people, products, and processes is necessary to prevent fires from existing?

In our third and final act, we're going to consider the small things you can invest in as an emerging executive. We'll take a long look at how politics is affecting your organization and how communication is or isn't flowing across the company, and we'll finish with my defining leadership principle.

19

Allergic to Wisdom

The first three months at a new job is a delicate time because you are in the "first impression zone" where, whether you like it or not, the judgment factor is impossibly high.

I was a new VP. Treading carefully in meetings. Listening carefully. Not making bold moves. This is my standard operating procedure and I normally follow it for three months minimum until someone says, "When are you getting started?"

I've learned to ignore my instant negative knee-jerk reaction to this observation. It's clear they want to see change; otherwise, why'd they hire me? I understand they want to see that change sooner than later, but I know two things. First, I've been doing nothing but *getting started with 90 days of intense observation*. Second, I've learned the *perceptions built in the "first impression zone" are instant and hard to change.*

There are other odd statements made by my new team in these early days:

Don't mention your prior company.

No one says it like that. They say, "We're a unique culture" and other phrases designed to support the notion that this group of humans is blazing a truly original trail. Another one:

No one has ever done this before.

They do actually say that, and they are partially correct. They are proud of what they've built and I'm proud to be there, but the idea that this amazing group of humans is going to invent it all as they go is a dangerous and inefficient strategy. There is hard work ahead, and while this group of talented humans has built a product that has everyone's attention, they are not going to invent *how* to produce it or *how* to lead.

Still, why the allergy to preexisting wisdom? I can explain, because I've been there.

A Circus of Failure

As I wrote back in the introduction to Act I, my first management role started with Tony at Netscape walking into my cubicle on a random Wednesday to ask me if I wanted to be a manager.

"Sure," I said.

Thus began a multiyear circus of failure.

Remember, *management isn't a promotion, it's a career restart.* And just like when joining a compelling new start-up, we begin with the following affirmation: "I need to look like I know what I'm doing even though I've never done it before."

There's wisdom there. Part of leadership is learning to demonstrate enough charisma and enthusiasm to convince the team that against impossible odds, we will succeed. This behavior is supported by the unspoken fact that your team initially assumes, "The leader has a plan and even if I don't understand it now, I have faith they know what they are doing."

My failures were vast. There were morale issues because no one understood the product strategy I produced. They went undetected. Vapid and unhelpful performance reviews were produced. By me. Weeks of lost productivity occurred because I leaked to the team news of a forthcoming reorganization that wasn't done for another three months. Infighting occurred because I was a conduit for gossip. This chapter, like all the chapters in this book, documents a chunk of the circus of failures and the lessons I've learned in the years since I became a manager.

Hindsight has taught me to cherish these hard lessons and surface them as I encounter similar situations. So now I'm at the new gig and they're saying, "You sure talk about your prior company a lot."

I sure do. It's why you hired me.

...is what I don't say.

When to Innovate and When to Iterate

The unintentional allergy a rapidly growing start-up has to preexisting wisdom is part ignorance and part pride. These start-ups are successful because they believe at their core that the impossible can exist. It's my favorite part of the culture and it's why I don't say, "Back at Apple, we did it this way." I just act without asking.

Their enthusiasm for this business they brought into existence has spilled over into all aspects of the organization. *Everything must be looked at through this innovative lens.* Sure, I'm a firm believer that we must continuously evolve ourselves and our business, but the act of innovation is an expensive one. We stop. We stare at the problem set. We debate. We debate endlessly. We yell. We whiteboard. And then finally we come to a clever, thoughtful, and defensible decision on how to proceed, and we charge forward enthusiastically because we just brought this unique decision, this perceived invention, into the world.

Every aspect of a rapidly growing, innovative company does not need to be processed through this innovation engine. In fact, you are going to lose valuable energy, momentum, and productivity doing so. There are a handful of company-critical decisions that need this level of attention, and for the rest we can rely on prior art.

I just act. I don't ask. I don't build consensus. I just go.

When I arrived at my most recent gig as the VP of Engineering, one of the first obvious areas of investment was the career path for engineers. We had an unfinished draft that was being used as a rubric for promotion decisions, and there was significant pressure to get a final draft.

I'd faced exactly the same issue at my prior gig. There, I gathered a group of engineers and managers together and we innovated. The committee spent seven months drafting, editing, vetting, and redrafting an excellent career path. It was ready for use a year after we began.

This year of investment was front of mind for me when the request arrived at the new gig. I asked myself, "Do I want to spend a year, thousands of engineering hours, on once again inventing a career path?"

If I were to ask the team, innovation bias would cause them to declare, "Of course, we're here to change the world!" So I didn't ask. I took a draft of a prior career path, I carefully weaved in what I'd discovered during my 90 days of exploring the company's culture, I shared it with one other leader, and then I declared, "This is our career path."

It was a B. It wasn't a work of art, but it was usable, instructive, and a good starting point. More importantly, it saved our company thousands of hours.

These were hours we instead spent building products and features and fixing bugs. Yes, we collectively could have made the career path artifact an A, but we got a majority of the value from the B and then we iterated.

Act Without Asking

There is an obvious significant risk in this small thing, and that's why I placed it in Act III of the book. Your team's first impression of your leadership style should not be, "My new executive is not going to ask my opinion. They like going rogue." I would much prefer, "My new executive moves rather quickly and with intense and defensible purpose."

The first 90 days is a dangerous time. First impressions are hard to change. Your first few months set the tone. Simple acts as a leader will resonate loudly throughout the team and the organization.

As an executive, you're in the unique position of being the human in charge of the entire organization. You have a boss. They're the CEO, but they're busy being the interface to the rest of the world and their expectations of you are something like, "Productively run your business. Competently answer questions when I ask them. If you need help, ask."

My default operating model is sharing a vision for where we're going. This means describing our ambitious future and all the strategic steps we'll need to take to get there. I'll want your opinion because I know ideas get better with eyeballs, but sometimes, rarely, we're just going to go. See, I've been here before and by acting without asking, I'm giving us a strategic advantage, I'm saving us time and money, and I'm being a leader.

See, managers tell you where you are. Leaders, all leaders, tell you where you're going.

20

The Guard

The Old Guard is the set of humans who inhabit the early days of a start-up. As I've written about before, they define the culture in both obvious and nonobvious ways. Simply put, the way they act and how they treat each other disproportionately affects the values of the company.

The Old Guard get to be the Old Guard because they are successful and the team grows large enough to allow for the existence of the New Guard. The New Guard are not initially defined by their ability, age, or experience; they are defined by when they are hired. They were not there in the formative early days of the company, and they start their jobs at a distinct cultural disadvantage.

I've arrived at my last three jobs at roughly the same growth inflection point: during the arrival, education, and integration of the New Guard. My job places me directly and strategically between these two populations, which is why much of my writing for the past decade has focused on debugging and documenting how each group works, what they value, and how they interact (or fail to).

And at each company, the following seminal meeting has occurred...

The Disaster Meeting

A disaster has occurred. The specifics aren't important. What is important is that neither the Old Guard nor the New Guard predicted the disaster. Everyone was surprised, so someone called a meeting. I can tell the magnitude of the disaster because *everyone* is invited: Old Guard and New.

The meeting begins. As they always do, someone from the Old Guard starts talking confidently about disaster remediation steps. Other Old Guard members chime in with helpful suggestions, and someone steps up to be whiteboard operator. *We are getting s—t done, people.*

After 10 minutes, a New Guard engineer, Jordan, raises her hand and asks, "Can we go around the table and introduce ourselves?" It is this moment that makes this meeting memorable.

The silence is deafening. It's the Old Guard realizing there are strangers in the room. That's never happened before. It's the New Guard breathing a mental sigh of relief: "Finally, I am invited to a meeting where I am going to figure out who these people are and what they do."

And it's me realizing, "Oh, these people don't know each other. They're not a team yet."

The Productive Team Teams

The core attribute of a productive team is so simple and obvious that we forget it—it's like breathing, an act so essential that we forget we do it, though we can't exist without it.

A productive team *knows itself.*

The team members know each other's names, and they understand and appreciate each other's respective strengths, weaknesses, and motivations. They are not strangers.

With this essential understanding in place, and with practice, the humans in a healthy team effortlessly and without ego call on each other when they need help. They do not care who gets the credit for the work because *they want the work to get done well by the most qualified humans with the best judgment.*

This is a team that trusts itself, and it is likely that you've spent most of your career not on this type of team. I'm sorry. Let's talk about some of the reasons this hasn't happened yet.

Learned Helplessness

The acquired mindset of the New Guard is one of disappointment. They wouldn't be here if they didn't believe in the dream that was built by the Old Guard. They've been here for a little while, but they don't feel like part of the solution. They are distant observers. They watch the Old Guard's borderline-magical ability to get things done. (There is no magic. Just context.) Each time they attempt to bring a new thing to the table the Old Guard quickly point out, "We already solved for that three months ago." (They haven't. They solved for one case...not all cases.) The New Guard do know people's names, but they don't know each other.

When you combine the New Guard's basic lack of familiarity with the people and the product with the Old Guard's incessant repetition of some version of the mantra "Sink or swim!" the entire team enters a phase of learned helplessness where their respective rallying cries are:

- Old Guard: "I feel empowered to fix *everything*."
- New Guard: "I don't know how to fix *anything*."

And things need fixing. Things are breaking in increasingly unfamiliar ways...faster. The Old Guard's facade of calmly informed control weakens as they realize their ability to fix the things is limited by their number. And they don't ask for help from the New Guard because, as the New Guard, they don't know who these people are.

The myriad ways a group of well-intentioned humans prevent themselves from trusting each other is just...mind-boggling.

Trust Falls for Everyone!

You know what the most-ridiculed team building exercise is for an offsite? Trust falls. The idea is that the team separates into pairs and each group performs an exercise where one person faces away from the other person, folds their arms, and falls backward—and hopefully, the other person catches them.

Trust falls are the rallying cry for the awkward offsite, but what makes them awkward? Why are they ridiculed? What about this exercise makes it funny? Trust? What's funny about that? Nothing. We giggle about trust falls because we don't really know the complex mechanics of building trust in a work setting.

The Old Guard trust each other because through a combination of luck, smarts, blood, sweat, and tears they managed to bring a new thing into the world. Most teams fail at this effort, but this team did not. They think and talk fondly of those years now. The tales they tell of those formative times are becoming the myth. *We were drunk at a bar, and Samuel threw out this throwaway feature idea. That's where this multibillion-dollar business came from...Sam's drunk thought.*

The Old Guard don't tell the story of when no one talked to each other for a week because of a disagreement over architecture. They don't talk about those long 72 hours where if funding didn't show up, they were done. They don't tell these stories because they hurt to tell; they are awful stories. But they are as important as the myths, because they resulted in the construction of trust within the team. *If we can get through that, we can get through anything.*

Our fundamental discomfort with relying on another human being—no questions asked—is one reason the Old Guard and the New Guard exist. Strangers don't trust each other. These two populations exist because they have not yet gone through the critical and often painful process of building trust.

But then Jordan raised her hand...

Never Waste a Disaster

"Can we go around the table and introduce ourselves?"

I jump in quickly because I've been in this meeting before and add, "Thanks, Jordan. Can you tell us who you are, what you do here, and why you're in this meeting?"

The disaster that forced this meeting is the beginning of a story about trust. The reasons this disaster occurred and the work we'll do preventing future disasters from occurring is less important than the fact that we are doing the work together.

There is no Old Guard or New Guard. There is just The Guard. What are we guarding? Why are we here? We're building approachable tools humans can use to ask hard questions of their data. We're building an infinite catalog of beautiful ideas. We're building a new way of working together as a team. Yeah, we're guarding those dreams, but we're also going to learn about guarding and protecting each other, because that's what teams do when they trust each other.

21

The Culture Creek

A winter ritual. California. Santa Cruz Mountains. No snow at our altitude, but normally a decent amount of rain that starts sometime around Thanksgiving and sticks around until March or so.

California mountains. In a redwood forest that has been shaped by running water for much longer than there have been humans building things. Building a house in the mountains means considering the land. Is it base rock? Is it clay? How much is it going to move when it shakes? A lot? Okay, then dig deep piers. Fill them with rebar and concrete and you have a solid foundation.

However, there is still water. When I say "water," you're probably thinking that stuff you drink. Maybe you're thinking of a large body of water near you. Maybe there are waves in this water. Maybe not. The water I'm talking about is the stuff that falls from the sky and then runs down the hill. A simple act that over hours, days, months, and years leads to erosion. It's the water grabbing loose stuff in the ground and bringing it along for a ride. Thanks, gravity.

Over periods of heavy rain, what was solid ground can become so saturated that it turns into a liquid. As a liquid, the former dirt, now mud, has a different relationship with gravity. It's called a mudslide.

Because we don't want our mountain homes sliding down the hill, we work to move all running water elsewhere. Roof gutters lead to spouts, which lead to pipes that divert rainwater away from the house. Roads funnel to drains, which do the same.

This is where I come in.

It's a rainy season tradition that in the middle of a big rainstorm, I put on boots, waterproof pants and jacket, and a wide-brim brown hat. I grab my favorite shovel and I wander our property looking for where water runoff is being hindered. Leaves, logs, really anything can stop a well-intentioned temporary creek.

You think I do this because I don't want my house slipping down the hill—and you're right. This is on the list of the reasons. But at the top of the list is the fact that I derive immense pleasure from the delicate craft of curating rivers and creeks. Today, I spent three hours hiking around both my property and, uh, everyone else's property making sure that creeks and rivers were flowing properly.

I've heard my favorite engineers claim the reason they are productive is because they are lazy. It's a humblebrag. These humans don't have a lazy bone in their bodies. What they appreciate is efficiency. *I want to design this system so I only have to do this once.*

Setting up the initial conditions and letting the work just happen.

Hike down one of these creeks, clear debris, open up a passageway for a small rivulet, and then just stare...for a very long time. Immense pleasure. I have a similar fascination with staring at a fire in the fireplace. My brain is wired to derive pleasure not just from the intricate fractal details of a running creek or a burning log, but from the fact that I can also see evidence of my own underappreciated productivity in these things.

I can see the water productively flowing down the hill, and I can also see the water that will flow. I know that at the end of the rainy season a small temporary creek will have carved a foot-deep cut in the ground. In another five years, Mother Nature will have made a small canyon here with the help of well-placed water, dirt, and gravity.

My responsibility: keep an eye on it. Sometimes I'll need a shovel. My ability to change the course of this runoff will decrease with each passing year, as the creek digs into the ground and grows.

I need you to remember this creek when you start a new job.

An Unchangeable Culture

My chosen profession for the better part of a decade has been arriving at a rapidly growing start-up with a hundred or so employees. I've tried being employee 20, and while the experience was invaluable, the risk profile I'll now accept in my ideal company is closer to employee 100. At this stage the company has likely proven its business and is ready to scale. Sign me up.

Recalling my recent experiences at three such rapidly growing start-ups, I can confidently state three things:

- As I mentioned in Chapter 19, each of these start-ups firmly believes the problem set it is facing is unique and will require novel solutions. They are mostly wrong.

- The humans already present at these start-ups have developed a unique and efficient bond amongst themselves that is nigh impossible to replicate with the new helpful humans who arrive. This is unfortunate.

- Most everyone is going to talk about how to build the culture, but the vast majority of the culture has already been built. No matter how many times a group of well-intentioned humans plasters a new set of values on the wall, the culture will not significantly change while the founding team is running the company. Really.

You might think the latter point is controversial and depressing.

Let's remember: this set of humans pulled off a miracle. Through an incredible amount of hard work, they've created a company. Not just any company, but one that is starting to look successful. They've had everyone they trust tell them it was impossible, they had to tell the half-baked story of their idea long before they had anything resembling a working product, and they had to attract others to their mission when they knew in their back of their minds the chances of success were low.

From these trials came a set of stories, and when you start a new job, your job is to listen for them.

Listen for the Stories

Your company's values are painted in huge black block letters on the wall. Let me guess:

- We Value Transparency
- Teamwork Makes the Dream Work
- We Are the Customer
- Be Kind
- We Are Obsessed About <Something>

Am I close? I bet I got at least one, and another is a mere synonym away from correct. The fact that there are similarities in start-ups' values isn't a surprise because all these companies are built by risk-taking, ambitious, slightly-off-kilter humans who love the challenge of bringing the new into the world...and they all face similar challenges. I love working with and learning from these folks, and one of the important lessons they've taught me over the years is that *the words on the walls are less important than the stories they tell.*

Listen. Maybe it's the first argument that you hear amongst the team. Perhaps it's a complicated design decision. No one is going to raise their hand and state a value: "We Are the Customer." Someone will tell a story. Here's what it might sound like:

> *Remember when AJ and Carol couldn't agree? Design and engineering. Going at it. They were in completely opposite corners and no matter how hard we tried to build the peace, they could not see eye to eye. We were about to call in the CEO hammer, but the moment they heard that they bolted. Out the front door—together—and they walked around the city until midnight. A six-hour 1:1. They came back to an empty office, moved their desks together, and worked all night on the design. When we came back in the morning, he was asleep under his desk, and she was off getting celebration donuts for the entire office because she knew we'd just successfully designed our most important feature.*

This story explains why there are donuts every Tuesday morning. This story also explains why AJ is now the VP of Product and Carol is now the VP of Engineering, but the reason they tell the story over and over again when the stakes are high at this hypothetical company is to remind everyone:

1. Engineering and design are equal partners.

2. There is a healthy tension in this partnership.

3. With it, we can do anything.

This is what actually happened. AJ and Carol did have a big fight that one time and they did leave, but it was because they were both attending a going-away party where they had a drink. They happened to discuss the feature in question. They discovered something and told people about that something (and brought totally unrelated donuts) the next morning.

However, you're going to hear the AJ and Carol story over and over again. It'll show up not just because it was a formative moment in the company's history, but because we bond over the stories we tell. It's how we connect and form the collective *us* from all the individual *I*s. A story is told and retold to remind us what is important. It will assist in answering hard questions. The stories that define a company remind us of what it took for us to get here. They shape the narrative and define the culture.

The Culture Creek

These stories are the culture. Not the words on the wall. It's convenient when the stories and the words support each other, but I've worked at companies where teamwork was preached as a core value—I heard about it during the interview process, it was an essential part of onboarding—but the first real story I heard over lunch was how the CEO was a horrific dictator.

The stories that define a culture are not a deliberate strategy. No one called a meeting to decide which stories mattered to the company. A core set of humans in the building retold *the stories that mattered to them*, over and over again, slowly carving a well-defined path in the consciousness of the company. With time, it becomes religion. When we're in situation X, we tell the tale of story Y. Does story Y always apply to situation X? Maybe. I don't know. It's the story we tell.

22

Anti-Flow

Being in the Zone is an essential practice for me. The Zone is a place, and Flow is an activity that occurs within this precious mental space. Flow is the ability to consider a project or a problem deeply. In Flow, you can keep a superhuman amount of context in your head and can traverse that context with ease. With Flow, you can produce extraordinary value. Flow is writing this chapter right now, but this chapter eventually needs another section, and, oddly, it's yet another activity within the Zone. I've started to call this activity Anti-Flow.

Anti-Flow is shower thoughts. They are the random connections your brain makes about a problem, a thought, or an opportunity when you *aren't* thinking about that problem, thought, or opportunity. The unexpected magical quality of these discoveries might give you the impression that the summoning exercise is equally magical, but I've discovered a simple process to create hours of fertile Anti-Flow.

Applied Anti-Flow

This chapter is currently 924 words. Six paragraphs. I think I've got the title and I can see in my head the arc of the piece. I don't have an ending yet, but it's likely going to repeat a mid-article point about the importance of Anti-Flow to your daily working life. Something about how the nonobvious work is as important as the obvious work. Yeah, that's good. Gosh, I love Flow.

In about a half-hour, I'm going to stop writing this piece, and I'm going to jump on my bike Isabelle, and we're going to go on a long ride. Three hours. Almost 40 miles.

Once I'm on my ride and I've biked a few miles, it is likely my brain will think about this piece automatically. *Good title? Yeah. Meaningful arc? Sure.*

Anti-Flow has a negative connotation. Is that a problem? Maybe I should research usage of the term? Good idea.

Predicting what might pop up during the ride is impossible because Anti-Flow, by definition, is about discovering hidden potential and strange connections in the strange mental crevices of your mind. If applied Flow is directing the creative process, Anti-Flow is about lack of direction to achieve an even more ambitiously creative end. An example: it is equally likely that once I start riding Anti-Flow will percolate a random idea about a meeting I had two weeks ago that ended badly. I haven't thought about this meeting since it ended, but my brain knows there is an open thread there and the legit magic of Anti-Flow is that—*bam*—here's a random thought on how to fix a problem I'd forgotten I had. Gosh, I love Anti-Flow.

My weekend morning process, I've discovered, is about creating Anti-Flow. No calendar staring at me, a quiet morning, coffee, and a blank browser page. No guardrails. Start stumbling around the internet and see what strikes. High creative entropy means I am in Anti-Flow. However, there is an equal chance that I'll head down a Wikipedia rabbit hole for an hour, continue writing an in-flight piece, or write something brand new. The moment I start building, I leave Anti-Flow and enter Flow.

On a long ride, there are no rabbit holes or keyboards. I can't engage a random idea because I'm sitting on a bike, which means *the high-entropy state of Anti-Flow persists*. My biggest challenge is remembering the random ideas that show up, so I've developed a simple system. If an idea shows up and I deem it worth further investigation,[1] I remember the one word that encompasses the idea and start making a memorable sentence. The sentence from a recent ride was, "Larry stats offsite in London." Gibberish, right? Two of those words were absolute gold.[2]

---

1 Yes, there are truly dumb ideas that show up that I briefly consider and then dump.

2 Wondering what I found during Anti-Flow on this ride? Well, I did edit this piece, but I was mid-mental edit when I found this beautiful vintage 1966 Toyota Stout 1900 and complimented the owner, who ended up buying me coffee and jelly beans. After that, I thought about the power of compliments combined with the appreciation of vintage things we've built with our hands. There's a chapter there. Speaking of chapters, I also started a piece in my head that I'm currently calling the Rands Information Diet™. I worked on a secret project. And I decided to remove every single thing from my bedside table except for the current thing I am reading. The sentence: "Watch independence Toyota music ledger stack."

Weaponized Inspiration Generation

As I look at my work calendar, I see comfortable boxes of time designed to chunk my week into knowable bits of time. Those bits of time are meetings where I and humans I care about have structured our time with agendas. Crafted to focus on the problems at hand, agendas are run by humans and keep us on topic and within time. These boxes are valuable. Decisions are made. Work that matters progresses in a structured fashion.

By design and with a lot of help, my week and my mind are on rails. There is essential unmeasurable work that needs to happen on a regular basis that should not just happen in the shower.

Anti-Flow is the weaponized generation of inspiration. Anything can show up during deep sessions of Anti-Flow, from the mundane to the magical. The title of this book showed up on a ride last summer. The single most important line for a recent talk arrived two weeks ago. The correct order of operation for telling a human very bad news arrived three weeks ago. One week later, I discovered the words that I needed to say.

Not knowing the source of this inspiration makes the concept of Anti-Flow at odds with a working day, which perhaps makes a bike ride a better place to Anti-Flow. It's one of the reasons why when my wife asks me, "Do you get bored on three-hour rides?" I respond honestly, "It's when I do my most important work."

You don't bike. That's fine. Think about the last time you had a non-shower *a-ha* moment. Cleaning the garage, knitting, driving to Monterey Bay. There were no internet distractions, and an intriguing idea appeared out of nowhere. Wherever you were, whatever you were doing, devise a reliable means to do it again. Every week. There is Anti-Flow to be had everywhere.

23

A Meritocracy Is a Trailing Indicator

As a manager, when a direct report asks, "What do I need to do to get to the next level?" I maintain that the quality and completeness of your answer is directly correlated to your effectiveness as a leader.

Let's start with the worst answer: "We're a meritocracy where the best idea wins."

This is a bulls—t cop-out answer. First off, being a meritocracy is a philosophy, it's not a strategy. Using this as an answer to a question about professional growth is akin to saying, "We give out gold medals when you win, so when you start getting gold medals, we'll all know you're winning."

A meritocracy, if achievable, would be a trailing indicator—a sign that long ago, your leadership team successfully created a culture where humans were recognized because of their ability. It reads like a noble dream worth striving for, but it is poor career growth advice.

Here's a better answer.

Two Paths

There are two career paths[1] in your organization: one that describes the growth of individuals and one that illustrates the growth of managers. These paths are readily visible public artifacts written by those who do the work. This means engineering writes the path for engineers, marketing writes the path for marketing specialists, and so on.

---

1 Some folks like using the word "ladder" here, but I prefer the term "path." A ladder is a thing you must climb upwards. A path is a journey.

The contents of these artifacts need to reflect your organization's values, culture, and language. For individual contributors, I humbly recommend the career path contain the following information:

A series of levels and titles
> A level is a generic number to differentiate each echelon, like Engineer 1, Engineer 2, etc. A title is a more descriptive version of the level, such as Associate Engineer, Engineer, Senior Engineer, and so forth.[2]

A brief description of the overall expectation of each level
> For a Senior Engineer, this could be: "Owns well-defined projects from beginning to end."

A list of competencies that are required for each level
> These are the measures of success. An example competency might be "Technical ability," and the career path might offer the following definition: "Designing, scoping, and building features and systems. Helping others to make technical decisions."

A definition of how each competency may be demonstrated, for each level
> For the technical ability competency, the description for an Associate Engineer ("Implements and maintains the product or system features to solve scoped problems. Asks for guidance when necessary.") will be much different than that for a Senior Engineer ("Independently scopes flexible technical solutions. Anticipates technical uncertainties. Trusted to design and implement team-level technical solutions. Guides team to improve code structure and maintainability. Garners resources required to complete their work.")

This suggested list is not definitive. You could easily add to this artifact items like a sphere of influence, ideal years of experience, or comparable levels outside of your company. And then do the whole thing over again for your manager career path.

If you are feeling overwhelmed by the enormity of this task, you're in good company. You can certainly find career paths online that can serve as starting

---

2 Yeah, I said that titles are toxic. In particular, I said: "The main problem with systems of titles is that people are erratic, chaotic messes who learn at different paces and in different ways." This is true. It's also true that I have not yet thought of a better mechanism for defining career progression.

points for creating these descriptions, but I strongly encourage your team to write their own because your culture is unique. The competencies you need are a function of the values of your particular collection of builders.

As a human who has screwed up the design and launching of career paths in every possible way, I have some hard-earned advice to share on common pitfalls.

Two Equal Paths

Let's start with framing. You need to make it clear that these two paths—management and individual—are equivalent. I'll explain this concept by describing how *not* to design your career paths.

The need for a career path begins when there are enough engineers to require a rubric for career growth. A well-intentioned group of individuals defines this path. Great! You have a career path. Who decides who goes where on this newly defined path? What level is everyone at? Who is "senior"? Usually some form of manager makes these decisions. It is at this moment when individual contributors not familiar with the ways of managers realize that these folks have a heretofore unknown influence on their careers.

When it becomes apparent these managers have special powers, a subset of individual contributors quickly become interested in management. The problem is that this is often a career path that doesn't yet exist, usually because those who would normally write this path were too busy working to define the individual contributor career path.

Here's the screw-up. You just finished defining the individual contributor career path, and suddenly everyone is interested in a career path that has yet to be written. What's up? The answer is, the individual career path has not made it clear that *individuals have equal opportunities to lead.*

There are many good reasons for an engineer to want to move into management, but if their only reason is the perception that management is the best place to grow as a leader, then the leadership team has created the perception that leadership is not the job of individuals. This is a disaster.

The Growth Tax

Artifacts like career paths show up to document the company culture, to define rubrics, and to help inform a process that will allow informed decisions to be made to help the team scale. These artifacts provide accessible definitions, but how they are applied is what the team is truly watching. In the example just described, where managers are choosing levels for a newly defined individual career path, each member of the team cares equally about their level and *who is choosing it.*

During a period of rapid growth with only organic role definition, everyone is wondering where they stand because everything is changing all the time. Suddenly, these new managers appear who have the power to determine roles, and individuals ask themselves, "What other powers are they going to grant themselves? And how do I get in on that action?"

So, you wrote a career path for individuals in which you defined a clear set of competencies signaling the growth of the individual—but you forgot to make it clear that leadership comes from everywhere. If an individual doesn't believe that they have the same ability to lead as a manager, then those who desire to lead will attempt to get on the manager path.

This isn't a horrible outcome because you do need capable managers, but it's a failure because you are signaling to your team that it's just the managers who are calling the shots.

One of the bigger challenges during rapid growth is a thing I call the *growth tax.* It's a productivity penalty you incur that increases as a function of the size of your team. Ask yourself these questions:

- How long does it take to make a hard decision?
- How does a person find out a critical piece of information?
- How do we figure out who owns what?

The cost to answer each of these (and far more) questions increases slightly as each new human arrives.

But these small communication taxes pale in comparison to the much larger taxes levied by defining cultural norms. By fostering the belief that the managers are the only leaders, you create hierarchy. *We must go to a higher power to ask for permission.* Hierarchy creates silos. *We own this, and they own that.* Silos often create politics. *Their mission is the only mission. Our mission is lesser.*

This is a disaster.

Leadership Comes from Everywhere

Meritocracy is a philosophy that states that power should be vested in individuals almost exclusively based on their ability and talent.[3] Advancing in this system is based on performance measured through examination and/or demonstrated achievement. As a manager and as an engineer, the concept of meritocracy is appealing. I want my teams as flat as possible and full of empowered individuals, and any action that reinforces the perspective that "managers have all the power" is suboptimal.

Are managers required as group size scales? My vote is yes. You might disagree, but I think having a set of humans responsible for the people, processes, and product is essential for scaling. One reason you might disagree is that you've seen managers who've done the job poorly. That sucks. There are good managers out there, and they are the ones who understand their job is to manage the health and advancement of their team, because without their team they have exactly no job.

The definition of individual contributor leadership starts with defining a leadership competency in your career path—but you need to spend an equal amount of time defining clear places for individuals to lead. Here are two roles you can invest in:

Technical lead

> What does "technical lead" mean for your company? Is it a throwaway title that managers use to placate cranky engineers? That's a missed opportunity to define credible contributor leadership. Here's a starting definition: "You are the owner of this code/project/technology, and this means you are the final decision maker when it comes to this area."

> With this definition in hand, make a list of all the technical areas that need technical leadership and make it publicly available. These are the areas we are responsible for, and these are the technical leads. Ask them first.

> Defining the numerous details of this role is potentially politically hazardous. For example, how long can someone be a technical lead? What

---

3 True story: while the concept of a meritocracy has been around for centuries, it wasn't until 1958 that humans called it a meritocracy. The term was coined by Michael Young, a British sociologist, who was satirizing the British education system. Young was "disappointed" that it was adopted into the English language with none of the negative connotations.

happens when they leave? And, finally, the contentious question: "Who chooses technical leads?" Sure glad we have managers to figure this out.

Technical lead manager

This role is a hybrid designed to give aspiring managers a transparent and fair view of people management. Technical lead managers continue to code a minimum of 50% of their time, but they also have direct reports. What's the catch? Cap their direct reports at three. This constraint is intended to give new managers exposure to all the aspects of people leadership (reviews, promotions, 1:1s—all covered in my book *Managing Humans*, Apress, 2016), while still giving them reasonable time to be hands-on engineers. Why three directs? Why 50%? Your ratios may vary, but what we're optimizing for is a higher probability that they can do both jobs well instead of both poorly.

Like with technical leads, the devil is in the operational details, but one cultural aspect I like to reinforce is the removal of any stigma when a technical leader manager chooses to leave the role. If after four months in this position they approach me and suggest, "I don't think I'm built for the people thing," I ask some clarifying questions, we discuss, and once we're both satisfied with the answers, we celebrate as they become an engineer again—because it's likely we just avoided inflicting another crap manager on the world.

A Trailing Indicator

My last piece of advice on career paths is the most complex and incomplete. As I wrote earlier, the manner in which you define leadership is as important as how you are applying it. A thoughtfully constructed promotion process provides a means of consistently and fairly demonstrating to the entire team how you value leadership.

The topic of building a promotion process deserves an entire chapter. I'll write it. I'm sorry to leave you hanging, but if you intend to follow the advice in this chapter, you're on the right track. You have career growth paths for both individual contributors and managers. You've also perhaps defined additional nonmanagerial roles that give individuals opportunities to lead.

The advice I've offered in this chapter will inform your future promotion process—both managers and individuals have been given a standard frame of reference to have career and promotion discussions not just at promotion time, but all the time. Your future promotion process also needs to answer the question, "Are you consistently and fairly promoting both individual contributors and managers who are demonstrating leadership?"

There is more work you need to do. You need to train your managers to have career conversations with individuals all year long, you need to build an employee-friendly internal transfer policy that allows individuals to freely move about your company, you need to invest in teaching the entire company to give feedback, and more. Building a growth-minded company isn't done by defining a word; it's done by hard work.

24

How to Build a Rumor

There's a rumor wandering through your team right now, and I'm sorry to report, it's toxic. It's the kind of rumor that stirs up so much interest and emotional energy that the humans can't help but repeat it to each other.

It's about you, and it's completely untrue.

When you hear the rumor, the content will provoke instant white-hot blinding rage, and you'll irrationally think, "I'm going to find the person who started this lie, and I am going to give them a piece of my mind!" Bad news. It is unlikely you'll ever know where this rumor came from—and worse, it's a certainty that it won't be the last toxic rumor to wander your halls.

When you calm down and are ready to listen, I have three stories to tell. I'll explain where many rumors originate and why they perpetuate, and I'll finish with a simple communication technique to combat them.

Gray Space

I've had this hypothetical meeting many times.

Joel, a peer, walks into the conference room upset. This scheduled-at-the-last-minute 15-minute meeting has no agenda. Joel starts, "Thanks for the meeting. I'm kinda freaking out."

"What's up? How can I help?"

"Chris [Joel's boss] was out last week. She canceled our 1:1 the week before, so I didn't know she was going to be out. That's two 1:1s that we've missed."

"Okay, but she's back today, right?"

"Right, and I'm pretty sure she's going to fire me."

"Whoa, two missed 1:1s and a crossed wire do not a firing make, Joel. There's something essential I'm missing here, right?"

There's not. The more questions I ask, the more I realize that based on two missed meetings and the fact that Chris forgot to tell her team she was going on vacation, Joel is concluding he is going to be fired. There is absolutely no clear rationale for Joel's opinion.

It's just plain old fear.

The fact is, in *the absence of information, your team will make up the worst possible version of the truth, usually reflecting their worst fears.* This deceptively simple rule is the reason for many of the rumors circulating within your team and at your company.

Being a part of rapid-growth start-ups for the past 10 years, I've had front-row seats for watching rumor cultures grow. It is during rapid growth that communication structures are tested. Each new human who arrives needs to understand the company, its culture, and its values. I'm talking about both the values you paint on the wall and the silent values that exist as a part of each team.

Overt and covert values are more easily infected and corrected before the organism reaches a size where the relatively new hires (the New Guard) outnumber the Old Guard. At this inflection point, the culture starts to drift because the amount of entropy introduced by the New Guard exceeds the ability of the Old Guard to correct it. This is when the fascinating rumors begin.

Rumors start in the gray space. This is the space created between rapidly growing teams that used to interact every day but are now sitting in different buildings. It's the space created by communication vacuums. You neglected to explain your intent regarding a strategic product decision. A single sentence at an all hands was misinterpreted, and no one raised their hand to ask for clarification. The rumor began as a simple misunderstanding, and then it became something much stronger and more pervasive. How?

Conformity

In 1951, Solomon Asch, a psychologist, conducted a series of experiments. Groups of eight participants were asked to complete a simple perceptual task. The reality was that seven of the eight participants were actors and were following a script. The eighth participant had no idea the others were actors and assumed everyone had free will.

The experiment was simple. Each participant viewed a card with a line on it, followed by another with three lines labeled *a*, *b*, and *c* (Figure 24-1).

Figure 24-1. Cards used in Solomon Asch's 1951 experiments in perception

Each participant was then asked to say aloud which line on the second card matched the length of that on the first card. As in the example shown here, all of the labeled lines were of clearly differentiable lengths. There was no trick to the cards. The trick was that the participant with free will would always answer last, which meant that they heard everyone else's answer before giving their own.

There were 18 trials, and in 12 of these the actors all picked the wrong line. Overall, 75% of the free will participants gave at least one incorrect answer during the 12 critical trials.

Again, there was no visual trick. Each test was as blatantly obvious as the one shown here. The trick is purely social. It's the unspoken pressure of being the one person out of eight who is wondering why in the hell everyone else is choosing the obvious wrong answer, and then caving to that pressure because, "Well, those other seven people must know something I don't."

The Asch conformity tests provide insight into groupthink. They demonstrate how we might choose an obviously erroneous path or explanation simply because the people around us have already done so. In my opinion, they also explain the means by which rumors move around an organization and gather strength.

Remember, in the Asch setup everyone is a stranger, and the question and the answer are obvious ("Can you pick matching lines?" "Yes."). When you hear an utterly bizarre rumor not once, not twice, but three times from *people you trust*, you start to wonder, "Well, there must be some truth there, right?"

The rumor likely started with just a hint of truth. There was a simple question to answer. But when it entered the communication tapestry of your organization, the truth vanished. As it was passed between trusted parties, the rumor gathered strength. The lie morphed and was reinforced by friends and coworkers who trust each other.

Rumors can be weapons. Rumors can change the course of history. But we are not talking about these vile instruments; we're talking about a misunderstanding, we're talking about a conversation misheard and then repeated in the hallway. And now we're going to talk about what you can do about it.

The Severity of Nonsense

Your brain is trained to detect bulls—t. Evolutionarily speaking, I don't know how we acquired this essential skill, but each human being can listen to a statement and make an initial assessment: "Bulls—t or not?"

In today's world full of robotic targeted micromessaging designed to match our worldview, we as a species are collectively super awful at bulls—t detection and prevention. But that doesn't mean you can't individually fight the power.

The difference between bulls—t and a rumor is the severity of the nonsense. Bulls—t sounds so insanely bizarre that it's easier just to ignore it, whereas a rumor often contains a semblance of truth that gives it a whiff of credibility. But whether it's a rumor or straight-up bulls—t, your response is the same: discover the truth.

A reminder: our hypothetical rumor is about you, which means upon hearing it your level of rage is going to be high. When that rage passes, you are in a unique position to triage this rumor because, lucky for you, you...are you. However this rumor has mutated in the hallways of your company, you are capable of mounting an informed defense because you are, hopefully, an expert on you.

The knee-jerk response to a rumor discovered is the indignant howl of the witch hunt victim: *WHO WOULD SAY SUCH A THING AND BOY AM I GOING TO GIVE THEM A PIECE OF MY MIND WHEN I FIND OUT WHO...* etc.

Chill. Scary but true rule: as a leader, at any given point during your tenure, 30% of your team is unhappy with your performance. It's not personal; it's simply that you are the leader in this situation. Even with a sound strategy, perfect judgment, and flawless execution of all your projects, a significant minority will be somewhere between unhappy and full of rage with regard to your performance. Your choice regarding project X was not their choice. You said a thing at a meeting that was not aligned with their values. It's an endless list of valid grievances. You will never know them all, but they exist. Right now.

Your witch hunt reflex is normal, because a good rumor is unintentionally designed to feel like a punch to the face. Rumors travel through the hallways of the corporation, refining their potency by being retold. In each retelling, a rumor is edited by the humans passing it on—and we humans love great stories. As a rumor travels from one human to the next, the story is embellished and improved. It's a cruel, efficient editing process unintentionally designed to give the story maximum dramatic effect.

And there's truth there.

THERE IS ABSOLUTELY NOTHING TRUE ABOUT THIS PUNCH-IN-THE-FACE RUMOR, LOPP! I HAVE NEVER I WOULD NEVER DON'T THEY KNOW THAT...etc.

Chill. There is a reason this rumor exists. There was some situation in the past that forced its existence, and the only useful thing you can do is stop and reflect on what truth is contained within its toxicity. I've watched a lot of witch hunts executed using "This isn't our culture!" as a justification. For toxic, abusive, or aggressively evil rumors, this course of action is justified, but most witch hunts do little more than fuel the rumor mill ("They're looking for witches!"). There is not one person who created this rumor; it was the whole team. Rumors are a function of culture.

Rather than stress uselessly about the source of the rumor or how it propagated, start by taking the time to reflect: What possible truth could be contained within the rumor? What unanswered question is this rumor trying to answer? It's about you, so what is the organism asking?

Your journey of self-reflection with regard to this particular rumor is a test. I'm not you, I don't understand your culture, and while I know contemplating, digesting, and understanding this rumor is rough, I also know you need to discover what, however inefficiently, the team is telling you.

What recent visible actions have you taken? What public comments have you made? Who was there? What did they hear? Yes, there is a nonzero chance that this rumor is a complete fabrication, but the rumor didn't die immediately. It traveled. It gathered strength as it moved in your direction, and there is also signal in that amplification.

It's possible you won't be able to discern the question being asked by this rumor. It's too far removed from its origin and has morphed into ridiculousness.

This means you get to mentally shrug and remind yourself that at least 30% of the team is unhappy with some or all of your performance.

A better result is that you find a hint of the question being asked. It can be a solidly structured hypothesis or a wild-ass guess, but with this insight in hand, you respond, and you act. You answer the question either in a public forum or with a change in your behavior. You release a little bit of truth into the wilderness.

Rumors Are a Function of Culture

This is how your rumor started. In a meeting two weeks ago, you said a controversial thing about an important topic poorly. Because you were in a hurry, you only stated half of your justification before you ran out the door. Your goal was to inspire, but for the folks who hadn't heard your pitch before, you mostly confused them.

One person in that meeting began an internal mental process that is the same process used for creative brainstorming—they began to theorize. *Did he mean this? Or that? What are the implications of this odd thing? Let's play those implications out. How do I feel about this? How do others feel? What does it all mean?*

Again, a normal and healthy internal mental debate motivated by a desire to understand. After a period of consideration, this human will have an epiphany. They come up with their best thesis, and it's an intriguing one because humans love great stories. They want to vet this theory with others, and they make the first of two choices: directly share with you or share with a trusted friend?

You're the boss. You're in a hurry. You're busy, so they choose the path of least resistance and talk with a trusted friend. As they are about to open their mouth, they make their second choice. Remember this thesis is about you, you're the boss, and it's juicy, so they don't start with "I think," they start with "I heard." The friend listens to the thesis, and they vigorously agree, which is interesting because *they weren't in the meeting.* They agree with their friend's enthusiasm for the thesis, not the facts. And they tell a friend. Who tells another friend.

Rumors are a function of culture. In this manufactured scenario, it was easier and safer to talk not to the originator of the situation, but to a distant observer. It was easier and safer to not stand behind one's words, but to attribute them to an anonymous other.

25

Kobayashi Maru Management

Ted's feeling pretty good. He sits across from me in the conference room and says, "Program launch is solid. We've been working on the details for almost a month. We vetted the concept with all the affected teams and made tweaks, and now they're fine. The only step left is sending the announcement to the whole company."

"Nice work, Ted," I say, "Huge amount of work."

"Thanks."

"You're not remotely done."

"Pardon?"

A Test of Character

In the 23rd century of the *Star Trek* universe, there exists a test for cadets on the command track of Star Fleet. Via Memory Alpha:

> *The test primarily consisted of the cadet placed in command of a starship. The ship would soon receive a distress signal from the* **Kobayashi Maru**, *a civilian freighter within the Klingon Neutral Zone that had been heavily disabled. Being the only ship in range, the cadet usually either chose to withdraw from the rescue mission or enter the neutral zone and rescue the vessel in risk of violating the treaties. The ship would then be confronted by Klingon battle cruisers which typically engaged in a firefight.*

The punchline? It is virtually impossible to win in this scenario. The cadet cannot simultaneously save the *Kobayashi Maru*, avoid a fight, and escape the Neutral Zone intact. The test is one of character and decision making.

A critical part of a manager's job lies in their ability to appropriately act in unusually complex, unexpected, and perhaps no-win scenarios. But you know what's better? Not getting into those situations in the first place.

A System Failure

The daily life of a manager is full of unexpected developments. The daily stand-up where you discover you're a month late on a feature. The 1:1 where Justin first tells you his shields are down. The random conversation in a hallway where you discover the first hint of an impending professional disaster. These discoveries are standard operating procedure, and they never stop. Good luck.

A Kobayashi begins innocuously. A simple communication. A nonhasty and thoughtful launch of a program. A well-designed and well-tested feature now available to 100% of your customers. You've done this before, and you're not worried. Which makes the reaction...jarring.

A Kobayashi erupts immediately. The swift response starts with someone raising their hand, virtually or otherwise, but what they say or type immediately differentiates this situation from your typical unexpected daily developments. You think, but do not say, "Oh. S—t."

Note

If you are finding this chapter uncomfortably vague and have no idea what I am talking about, I humbly suggest you stop reading right now because the rest of this chapter will continue to read as vague and unhelpful.

A Kobayashi is a system failure, and you understand this when the first bit of feedback arrives and it's a combination of:

- A complete surprise

- An intense adverse reaction

- Via a population of humans raising their hands in protest whom you did not expect

- Including a new piece of critical information you had no idea belonged in this situation

A Kobayashi is a system failure because the usual means of getting important work done in a group of humans has *failed spectacularly*. A reorganization that felt obvious and noncontroversial. An HR program that appeared to be a win for everyone. A well-intended disclosure of information planned to build trust on the team. The potential situations are endless, and the only true consistency is the two words. Your words.

"Oh. S—t."

A Perfect Kobayashi

The unfortunate truth of Kobayashis is that the best way to prepare for them is to experience them. Let's walk through a hypothetical scenario. Suppose I'm about to launch a new program. All good projects have a code name, so let's call this one The Good Place.[1]

These are the hypothetical specifics of The Good Place. It's a company-wide program I'm launching later this month. It should only affect 5% of the engineering team, and their day-to-day lives will be mostly unaffected for a quarter. After that, they'll need to make some changes to how they work, but hey, they have three months to prepare. No problem.

The Good Place shares attributes with all Kobayashis. Specifically:

- It affects a broad set of diverse humans.
- It represents an unfamiliar or significant change to how those humans work.
- Its *initial perceived* success depends on how the affected humans react to the change.
- It *looks* a lot like work I've done in the past.

Combined, those attributes create the perfect Kobayashi. My guard is down, the change is hard to digest, and I've underestimated the number of affected humans. Since success is dependent on initial perception, when that larger-than-expected reaction emerges, I go into extreme denial and start lying to myself:

- It's just a couple of people. *It's not.*
- It's just a misunderstanding. *It's not.*
- It'll blow over. *It won't.*

This is The Bad Place.

---

1 My current favorite show and a positive affirmation.

A Proper Preparation

A useful piece on how to move into damage control mode and deftly handle this no-win scenario seems like a good idea, but wouldn't it be better if this chapter explained how to not get into this situation in the first place?

Super.

My Kobayashi prevention protocol is, conveniently, the same process I follow for *any* significant change on the team. Let's begin:

1. *Frame the situation via a written artifact.* You need to create a presentation or document that clearly explains what is going on, why it is happening, what success looks like in light of this change, how you are going to measure success, and how anyone can give feedback on this development. This is simply a draft, and it's going to change a lot before you're done.

2. *Vet the draft plan with three no-skin-in-the-game trusted humans.* Take your draft and give it to three humans who are not affected by this change and whom you trust to tell it to you straight. If there is only one piece of advice you should follow in this entire chapter, this is it. Unaffected trusted humans are the ones who are most likely to both see the obvious flaws in your plans and be eager to tell you about these flaws.

3. *Write down a list of all people and teams that you expect will be affected by the change.* This exercise is the first step of building out a communication plan, but right now it's a sizing exercise. Write the list. How many folks are on it? Five? Just five? Why are you still reading this article if we're talking about five affected people? I'll tell you why. You can smell the larger-than-expected impact. Your Spidey-sense is tingling. How many humans will really be affected? Not just directly, but indirectly? Humans who care about the directly affected humans. Humans who will have a strong opinion about the change. Humans who are going to raise their hands and speak. Yeah, put them all on the list. Then return to your three trusted humans and vet the list.

4. *Draft your communication plan.* With your framing and vetted list in hand, it's time to operationalize this program. It's called a *cascading* communications plan because you start with the most affected humans and slowly work your way toward the less affected humans. Here's the order of operation:

a. A preflight meeting with affected humans in a 1:1 situation. Face to face, you are going to walk each directly affected human through the framing. The rule is: *no one who is directly significantly affected by this change can learn about this from anyone but you.*[2] I call this preflight because there is a nonzero chance that one of these humans is going to point out an obvious flaw in your plan. I'm not talking about being unhappy about the plan; I am talking about a strategic error in your framing and/or rollout. Plan for changes to your framing.

b. A walkthrough of the framing with small groups of "persons of interest," with Q&A. It's a little less personal in a group setting, but the goal is the same: gauge reaction and, if necessary, make adjustments to the framing.

c. A presentation with Q&A to affected teams, either team by team or all at once. By this point, you will have vetted the plan with trusted advisors, affected humans, and persons of interest. This is the first presentation where you are unlikely to make changes based on feedback from the audience.[3] At this point in the process, the questions that show up during Q&A will be ones you've heard a couple of times. Nailed it.

d. An announcement to the entire team or organization, depending on the size of the program, via a presentation, an email, or Slack.

Have you ever sat at your computer with a huge message that you need to send to the team in front of you and found you can't hit the Send button? You know why? You smell the Kobayashi potential of this message. You can sense there is an essential angle that you did not consider. There is one person who has critical feedback that you have not heard. You will know that you've done everything you can regarding Kobayashi prevention when it's trivial to hit Send. This is The Bad Place.

---

2 This rule does not scale. If you're launching a massive reorganization that's affecting hundreds of people, you cannot personally talk to every affected human. You *can* make sure that affected teams hear about the change well before the public announcement.

3 If surprises are showing up here, I bet you skipped a step.

A Prediction of the Unpredictable

Like with most principled leadership applied with consistency, your reward for all of this Kobayashi Maru inoculation is nothing. *Nothing happens.* No one raises their hand. There is no drama. The team looks at your framing, crinkles their foreheads, and then says, "Yeah, that makes sense. What's next?"

No one celebrates when nothing happens. We all know when something significant goes wrong, because suddenly everyone's rushing around with great ferocity. Heroes and heroines appear when something goes wrong. They work for three days straight. We award spot bonuses for this exceptional effort. There are no spot bonuses for averted disasters, because they are the result of capable leaders competently doing their jobs.

I, like Captain Kirk, don't believe in the no-win scenario in business. There will always be system failures, large and small, in complex groups of humans combined with rapidly changing stacks of technology. But there is a win inside each failure, because within each one there are discoverable lessons—and these lessons are essential new additions to the playbook we use to prevent such a failure from happening again.

That's how you win.

26

The Signal Network

I spend a lot of time listening. A nontrivial act for me because my mind...it wanders. However, I've got a system. Feet flat on the ground, slightly clenched jaw, staring you straight in the eyes. *I am full-body listening.* You have my complete attention. I am not missing a word.

We humans are experts at instinctively knowing where attention is focused. In a 1:1 situation, all it takes is a subsecond glance at my watch to indicate to the other party that my focus is elsewhere. I am not listening. In that instant, the quality of discourse plummets because the listening contract is broken.

My educated guess is that 50% of my job as a manager is information acquisition, assessment, and redistribution. It is my primary job, and the efficiency with which I do this directly contributes to the velocity of the team.

Critical Freshness

In thinking about all the listening I've done and information I've acquired, I discovered I have a mental model for classifying information. Figure 26-1 shows what it looks like.

This grid has two axes. The vertical axis measures the *criticality* of a given piece of information. Critical information might look like:

- Jake is about to quit.

- The arrival rate of critical bugs is rapidly increasing.

- A meeting just finished between engineering and sales where they were at each other's throats. Nothing was resolved. Everyone left the meeting mad.

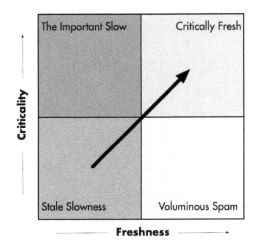

Figure 26-1. Grid for determining criticality and freshness of information

The horizontal axis is where this graph gets interesting. It measures *freshness*, which is a synthetic measure of how long it takes a given piece of information to get to the human *who gets the most value from its arrival*. Confused? Keep reading.

The interpretation of this graph is a very personal thing. You need to consider it as a thought experiment through a couple of different lenses. First, what is critical information to one human is irrelevant to another. Jake's desire to quit is hugely important to his manager, but less relevant to someone outside of the organization. Second, and worse, if the information about Jake takes two weeks to get to Jake's manager the information is not fresh, and Jake's manager has less time to take proper action.

Every single human in the organization has their own version of this graph, and my thesis is that the interpretation of the graph describes the health of your signal network.

Your Signal Network

Your signal network is the combination of all the available information sources and all the information generated (or relayed) via those sources. The complete network is a combination of humans and robots, but for the sake of this chapter, let's focus on human information sources. Back to the graph.

If you think about your average workday, you are continually discovering pieces of information. Intentionally and accidentally. In meetings, in hallways, and in the cafe. Your working life is chock-full of rapidly arriving information, and your brain must quickly digest, parse, pattern match, and make a judgment regarding each piece of information. What is it? How critical is it? What am I going to do with it? Should I pass it along? And to whom?

Each quadrant of this graph describes a different assessment of a piece of information. Let's walk through them:

Stale Slowness

The lower-left quadrant is the most boring one. The information here is not relevant and isn't fresh, but who cares? It's low-signal information, and it's stale, so there is no need to act.

Voluminous Spam

The lower-right quadrant is less annoying. You're still dealing with less-critical information, but the more you move to the right, the fresher the information is. You're sure learning lots of useless things quickly. At an extreme, it's spam. An organization spends energy moving information hither and fro. If you're seeing a lot of information falling into this quadrant, I am concerned about the overall efficiency of your team. If you're seeing a lot of useless information on a day-to-day basis, what about the rest of your team? How much time is the team spending wading through the noise to find signal? How much time is it wasting looking for nuggets of relevancy?[1]

Critically Fresh

The upper-right quadrant is your informational sweet spot. Critical information is getting to you in a timely fashion. Yes, it'd be super if all the information were further up and to the right, but the fact the information is in this quadrant is a win. The vibe here is a distinct lack of surprises. When a piece of information lands on your plate, it's fresh. It's clear someone just made this horrible decision, and you have ample time to coach them in the correct direction.

---

1 Gossip. Briefly, some information that shows up is gossip. It's half-informed opinion relayed as fact. Gossip is a trigger for me because it's often a precursor to the worst kind of politics, but gossip is signal. Rather than becoming angry—rather than wasting time on figuring out "Who would say that?"—I choose to dissect the gossip: What perfectly reasonable question is being asked with this inflammatory chunk of gossip? What observation is being made? This approach does not always work.

The Important Slow

The final quadrant, the upper left, is the danger zone. Critical information making its way slowly to the humans who need it the most is the source of much of your organizational consternation, and I need a whole section to explain why.

No Surprises

Members Only was the code name of one of my managers from The Start-Up You've Never Heard Of, and he exhibited many classic management tropes. We didn't know what he did all day, he practically never scheduled 1:1s, and when they were scheduled they were often rescheduled into nonexistence without notice. And when you finally got him pinned down in a meeting room, when you cornered him with the vital issue, he leapt to the first conclusion that crossed his mind and stated it as a fact.[2]

Members Only was fond of simple, pithy management proclamations that made a lasting impression on me. He told me one the first week he joined: "No surprises."

My interpretation of these two words from Members Only was not generous. What I heard was, "Make sure I know what's up, so I don't look bad." What he *might* have meant (but I'll never know) was, "Make sure our team of humans has the best information as quickly as possible so they can make the best decisions as quickly as possible."

Information consistently falling into the Important Slow quadrant means there are surprises. You're discovering unexpected developments occurring within the team *long after they happened.* You're unable to react because the time to act has passed. The conclusion is already history.

You can spend a lot of time and money investing in processes, tools, and artifacts that you believe are necessary to critical and timely information flow, but where I consistently invest is in the team. I demonstrate to the humans the value of effectively detecting, assessing, routing, and retransmitting information across the organization.

---

2 Much of the initial material for *Managing Humans* was created during this period.

High-Signal Humans

I have an internal measure that grades the following on any given day: How much critical information did I discover? And how fresh is it? In a rapidly growing organization of humans, the volume of new information created daily increases daily.

If you buy that ensuring the healthy flow of information is an essential practice as a leader, then you understand why I religiously hold 1:1s. It's a regular meeting where I make it clear what critical information I care about and where I consistently share the critical information my team needs. It's never a perfect transaction. I often incorrectly flag as essential information that is spam, and you will too. Over time, we will calibrate. In time, we won't wait until the 1:1 to relay information because we'll intuitively understand that for this given piece of information, the faster it lands in the right hands, the higher the value.

Your ability to effectively lead is a function of the collective quality of the decisions you make on a daily basis. You can take your time on many decisions. You can wait days or weeks until you've gathered all the relevant signal necessary. Other decisions must be made *right now*. At that moment, the health of your signal network, the amount of critical information that has arrived in a timely fashion, makes the difference between an informed decision and the flipping of a coin.

The health of your signal network is one lens into the health of your team. Critical information freely moving around the organization decreases surprises, improves the quality of decisions, and builds trust. Your team is your signal network, and you are theirs. Find and cultivate the high-signal humans.

27

A Precious Hour

I am told that the manner by which others understand that I am busy is when my writing coherence suffers. This primarily occurs in emails, when whole words are dropped, sentences become jumbled, and logic falls on the floor. Rands, I literally did not understand what you were asking in that email.

Poorly written emails are an early warning of intense busyness. Yes, I lack the time to proofread an email, but the mail is sent. At least I accomplished something. The step beyond this is when s—t is truly falling on the floor, and while s—t on the floor is professionally unacceptable, there used to be a point of irrational pride in my head when this situation occurred: look at me, how important I must be, with all the...busy.

It's this irrational pride I want to examine, because hidden inside of it is an insidious red alert situation.

The State of Busy Is Seductive

7:15 a.m. I sit down at my desk, fire up my calendar, and examine my day. Six meetings, starting in 45 minutes. All are compelling, all are likely to lead to progress. Good. Switch to Things and examine the backlog. I've got 45 minutes and 23 open tasks. Which of these should I prune? Which of these stay...Say, I've been meaning to call Joe for a week. I'll call him now.

7:25 a.m. Joe and I are on similar morning caffeination plans, so the call is high bandwidth. We're done with our three topics in 10 minutes, and I'm now sporting the rush of not just completing a task, but completing it at speed. I need to parlay this intense rush—what's next? Where else can I exceed my productivity expectations?

7:30 a.m. Okay, now I'm rolling. I've skimmed my emails and as I think of them, I'm writing tasks on a paper next to my keyboard, because I've somehow convinced myself that writing the task down on paper is faster than putting it in Things. (Huh?) No matter—all hail the rush of getting things done. The cycle continues. Another task is knocked off, a sip of coffee, and now I'm headed into my 8 a.m. with a head full of palpable busy.

The Zone is a well-understood mental state where you are fully dedicated to the problem that's in front of you. First you take the time to get the complete state of the problem in your head, which then allows you to make massive, creative mental leaps using a precious type of focus that is fleeting. In the 45 minutes leading up to my 8 a.m. meeting, I did not get in the Zone. However, don't tell my brain because I've worked hard to create the illusion that I am: massive amounts of data flowing about, a sense of purpose, and scads of coffee...but I am not in the Zone. I'm just busy.

The Faux-Zone

When an engineer becomes a lead or a manager, they create a professional satisfaction gap. They observed this gap long before they became a lead, asking themselves: "What does my boss do all day? I see him running around like something is on fire, but...what do they actually *do*?" The question gets personal when the freshly minted manager begins to understand that life as a lead is an endless list of little things that collectively keep you busy, but in aggregate don't make you feel like you're making much progress.

The positive feedback an engineer receives in the Zone is the sensation that you literally performed magic. From the complete problem set in your mind combined with your weapons-grade focus, you build a thing that you immediately recognize as disproportionately valuable. And you can see this value instantaneously—that's the high.

I believe that leads and managers are forever chasing the high associated with the Zone, but rarely achieve it because their job responsibilities directly contradict the requirements to get there. We often lack the time to gain the requisite intimate knowledge of a problem space because we rarely have 10 or 15 minutes free to consider it.

The amazing set of skills we've built to compensate for this utter lack of context is impressive. You would not believe how many times your boss has walked into a meeting with absolutely no clue what is supposed to happen during that meeting. Managers have developed aggressive context acquisition skills. They walk into the room and immediately assess whose meeting it is, then listen intensely for the first five minutes to figure out why they're all there while sporting a well-rehearsed facial expression that conveys to the entire room, "Yes, yes, I certainly know what is going on here."

Like these context acquisition skills, we've also convinced ourselves that we have built a mental process that gives us the high that we're missing in our interrupt-driven lifestyles. We've created *the Faux-Zone*.

In the 45 minutes before my 8 a.m. meeting, I did not enter the Zone, but I am in the Faux-Zone. It is a place intended to create the same rewarding sense of productivity and satisfaction as the Zone, but it is an absolutely fake Zone—complete with the addictive mental and chemical feedback, but lacking creative value. In the Faux-Zone, you aren't really building anything.

A Precious Hour

As a frequent occupant of the Faux-Zone, I can attest to its fake productive deliciousness. There is actual value for me in ripping through to my to-do list. I am getting important things done. I am unblocking others. I am moving an important piece of information from Point A to Point B. *I am crossing this item off...just so. Yum.* However, while essential to getting things done, the Faux-Zone is not a replacement for the actual Zone, and no matter how many meetings I have or how many to-dos are crossed off...just so. The sensation that I am truly being productive, that I am building a thing, is false.

My deep-rooted fear of becoming irrelevant is based on decades of watching those in the tech industry around me doing just that—sitting there busily doing things they've convinced themselves are relevant, but that really are just Faux-things-to-do wrapped in a distracting sense of busy. One day, they look up from their keyboards and honestly ask, "Right, so what's Dropbox?"

Screw that.

Other than spending time with my family, my absolute favorite time of the week is Saturday morning. I sleep in a little bit, walk upstairs, start the coffee process, and wander over to the computer. There's a Dropbox folder titled "Latest Rands Articles," and right at this moment there are 65 articles in progress there. After a brief stumble through the internet, a precious time begins. I have precisely the right music on, in the center of my screen is a wall of words, and in that moment I'm decidedly not busy, I'm not working—I am building a thing, and I need this time every single day.

Starting at the beginning of February, I made a change. Each day I blocked off a precious hour to build something.

Every day. One hour. No matter what.

Every day? Yup. Including weekends.

An hour? Yup, 60 full minutes. More if I can afford it.

Doing what? The definition of "building a thing" is loose. All I know is that I get rid of my to-do list, tuck the iPhone safely away, and if there is a door, I close it. Whether it's an hour of choose-your-own-adventure Wikipedia research, an intense writing session, or endlessly tinkering with the typography on the site, it's an hour well spent.

No matter what? Since I've started I've had roughly a 50% success rate in actually getting to my hour. The excuses are varied, but the data is compelling. Even at a 50% hit rate, I've written more, I've tinkered more, and, most importantly, I've spent over eight hours this month alone exercising the part of my brain I care about the most: the part that allows me to create.

What would you create if you had eight uninterrupted hours—every month?

An Insidious Situation

There is a time and place for the purposeful noisiness of busy. The work surrounding a group of people building an impressive thing contains essential and unavoidable busy, and you will be rewarded for consistently performing this work well. This positive feedback can feed the erroneous assumption, "Well, the busier I am, the more rewards are forthcoming." This is compounded by the insidious fact that part of being busy is that you aren't actually aware that you're busy because you're too busy being busy. You have no internal measurement of the amount of time you've actually spent being busy.

In my precious hour, I am aware that it is quiet. During this silence, maybe nothing at all is built other than the room I've given myself to think. I break the flow of enticing small things to do, I separate myself from the bright people on similarly impressive busy quests, and I listen to what I'm thinking.

Every day, for an hour, no matter what.

28

Find a Mentor

"Get the f—k out of there, Lopp."

Startled. I was startled. I was not expecting this advice. Months later I realized it was this very descriptive advice at this precise time from this specific human that helped me "get the f—k out of" that place at the right time. That surprising, colorful, and helpful bit of advice was from my mentor. His name is Marty.

The act of choosing a small thing to learn and practice is the easy part. The difficulty arrives in discovering for yourself why a particular small thing speaks to you. I knew and had been told for years that I needed to find a mentor, but it wasn't until I was a first-time director—when my situation was truly heinous—that I acted on the idea.

What Could Go Wrong?

First-time director. I'd been promoted because I'd written a couple of leadership books and had developed a strong support network of bright humans within the current company. They were looking for fresh blood, but the role was poorly defined and not running an engineering team. What could go wrong? Quite a bit.

While the leadership skills I'd built over the years were helpful, there was no way to quickly gather the immense domain context of a different job like, say, human resources. I was capable of leading, but the gaping hole in domain-specific experience caused the gig to go sideways within six months. I adopted the advice I'd readily given to many others, but had not yet followed. I hired an external human—who would eventually become my mentor—to do a 360 review of my performance.

A 360 review proceeds as follows:

1. You hire an external consultant. You need a neutral party.

2. You provide the consultant with a list of coworkers. These are humans who work for you, peers, your manager, and, if appropriate, their peers. This is where the term 360 comes from. You're interested in the perspective and experiences of all types of humans in your professional sphere.

3. The consultant interviews all of these humans. They pose the same set of questions to all the interviewees and probe two areas: What is Lopp doing well? Where does Lopp need help?

4. The consultant anonymizes and aggregates the interview feedback and then walks you through the results of the 360. In my case, I was presented with a printed document with two columns. Column A: Where Lopp is doing well. Column B: Where Lopp needs help.

Want to know why I preach about 1:1s? Want to know why I keep harping on the importance of feedback? It boils down to the moment I received the feedback from my first 360, and it was delivered by my future coach, Marty.

Sucker Punch

Marty sat across from me in my office. He handed me a printout of the anonymized and aggregated feedback and said, "You're going to want to read the hard stuff first, but let's first read the good stuff."

There was good stuff there. Familiar compliments I'd heard before, along with new ones. The "doing well" section filled a single page. The "needs help" section filled three pages. Reading through that feedback taught me an important and lasting lesson: we human beings are horrific at constructive face-to-face feedback.

Marty's individual interviews were 30 to 60 minutes long. He spent time understanding the feedback, digging for specifics, and clarifying so that he could effectively represent the feedback to me. He had the benefit of multiple perspectives, so when he heard recurring themes, he could dig even deeper for clarity because he knew this wasn't one person's opinion, but the team's. As an empathetic human, he also knew which feedback was going to sting, so he'd dig in there to make sure he'd be able to answer my inevitable questions.

When we finished reading the good stuff, we started on the hard stuff. Marty's advice at this juncture: "Read the whole thing without stopping. Remember to breathe."

Like the good stuff, the areas for improvement were not complete surprises. Nothing in column B was feedback I hadn't heard or considered in the past year. Presented in aggregate, though, it gave me a clear picture of how my team felt I was performing...perhaps for the first time in my career.

A small word spoken during that staff meeting. The discussion I had two weeks ago when a trusted someone was dancing around the actual feedback. The strange vibe in that meeting that was created when I raised my hand to volunteer for that project. *Too much on my plate. Doesn't say no. Conflict averse. Lossy when stressed.* Column B was the single most concentrated set of feedback I'd received in my life.

Marty did a masterful job of walking me through it. When I asked for clarification on feedback, he clarified. When I asked about the priority or severity of a piece of feedback, he provided it without betraying confidence. He'd heavily edited the feedback to anonymize it so I didn't obsess about one person's opinion on my team. He made the feedback entirely about me.

It was exhausting. Then Marty said, "Sleep on it. Think about it. Let's meet again in a week, because that's when the real work starts."

Marty taught me the phrase, "Feedback is a gift." The phrase is designed to remove the fear of receiving critical feedback, to reinforce the fact that you are about to receive a useful thing. I've discovered another interpretation of it, too. See, the important part of feedback isn't just that you receive the gift; you also need to unwrap (or unpack) it.

At our second meeting, Marty and I walked through my digested and constructive thoughts regarding the feedback. The goals of this meeting were to answer any lingering questions and to figure out how I was going to proceed.

"Marty, there's a lot here. I'm not sure where to start."

"Lopp, pick the most important thing."

"Marty, what do you think it is?"

"It's the most important thing to you."

You will notice Marty did not answer my question. He turned it around. He had *me* answer the question. This is a good time to remind you this chapter isn't about the value of feedback, it's about *finding your mentor.*

My Mentor Requirements

I am not you, so what I look for in terms of a mentor may be different than what you need. The reason I started this piece with the 360 is because if you don't already have a mentor, a 360 can give you the beginnings of a map that will show you the areas you need to work on, which will lead you to your mentor. In my case, I needed someone who could help me speak and find truth.

As an introvert, I am worldclass at avoiding saying anything. I have a rich set of communication tools designed to get you talking. It's not that I don't have topics to discuss, it's that the act of speaking is an uncomfortable one for me. It's far easier to step back, let you talk, and then react to what you are saying. Turns out these communication tools often translate into good leadership skills. Go introverts.

Marty gets me talking. This is work because I'm built to listen. My first official post-360 sessions with Marty were full of painful silence. He'd ask me a question and I'd flip it and turn it back to him and he'd say nothing. The question was for me to answer.

And he'd wait.

He'd wait some more.

We'd stare at each other, he'd smile, and I'd finally answer the question because this was a time for me to sort through my thoughts. It certainly matters what Marty thinks, but the reason we were sitting there was to dig up my thoughts, critique them, and then figure out the work that needed to be done.

The first work that Marty and I did was to get me to stop redirecting all my attention elsewhere and focus it on me. How did I feel about the feedback? Where did I think I needed to improve? And what was I going to do about it?

"Get the F—k Out of There"

This was advice Marty gave me years later. Two jobs later. Unlike in our former exploratory discussions where the conversation was deliberately circuitous, this advice was clear, colorful, and direct. When he arrived in my office, I gave him the lowdown on the current situation as objectively and fairly as I could. I walked through various strategies I'd considered, and Marty dropped the bomb.

Why then? Why after years of coaxing thoughts out of me, finding the truth, and working on a focused plan of actions did he suggest this drastic course of action?

He just skipped the first three steps of the process because he's my mentor. He understood after years of conversation that there were no new thoughts to be discovered, no truths to be defined; it was time to act. I can count on one hand the number of humans with whom I have this type of high-trust relationship.

A trope about leadership is that it's lonely at the top. Your responsibilities as a leader of humans require you to define a clear, professional distance between yourself and your team. You can be friendly, but not friends. This is mostly true.

Don't confuse this professional distance with distance from everyone. You need insiders. High-bandwidth insiders who know the entire story. You need them for the same reasons you need a diverse team. Different perspectives create well-informed debate, which allows for better decisions.

And, remember, you are a leadership work in progress.

29

How to Rands

Hi, welcome to the team. I'm so glad you are here at $COMPANY.

It's going to take a solid quarter to figure this place out. I understand the importance of first impressions, and I know you want to get a check in the win column, but this is a complex place full of equally complex humans. Take your time, meet everyone, go to every meeting, write things down, and ask all the questions—especially about all those baffling acronyms and emoji.

One of the working relationships we need to define is ours. The following is a user guide for me and how I work. It captures what you can expect out of the average week working with me, how I like to work, my North Star principles, and some of my, uh, nuance. My intent is to accelerate our working relationship with this document.[1]

Our Average Week

We'll have a 1:1 every week for at least 30 minutes, except during HIGH ALERT (see below). This meeting is for discussing topics of substance, not updates. I've created a private Slack channel for the two of us to capture future topics for our 1:1s as well as to provide a handy historic record of what we've discussed. When you or I think of a topic, we dump it in that channel.

We'll have a staff meeting with your peers every week for 60 minutes, no matter what. Unlike for 1:1s, we'll have a shared document that captures agenda topics for the entire team. Similar to in 1:1s, we aren't discussing status at this meeting, but issues of substance that affect the whole team.

---

1 Speculation: There is an idea in this document that you'd like your manager to do. Thesis: Just because I have a practice or a belief doesn't mean it's the right practice or belief for your manager. Suggestion: Ask your manager if they think my practice or belief is a good idea and see what happens. Feedback is a gift.

You can Slack me 24 hours a day. I like responding quickly.

If I am traveling, I will give you notice of said travel in advance. All our meetings will still occur, albeit with time zone considerations.

I work a bit on the weekends. This is my choice. *I do not expect that you are going to work on the weekend.* I might Slack you things, but unless the thing says URGENT, it can always wait until work begins for you on Monday.

I take vacations. You should, too. When I'm disconnected from work is when I do some of my best work.

North Star Principles

Humans first. I believe that happy, informed, and productive humans build fantastic products. I optimize for the humans. Other leaders will maximize the business, the technology, or any other number of important facets. Ideological diversity is key to an effective team. All perspectives are relevant, and we need all these leaders, but my bias is toward building productive humans.

Leadership comes from everywhere. My wife likes to remind me that I hated meetings for the first 10 years of my professional career. She's right. I've wasted a lot of time in meetings that were poorly run by bad managers. As an engineer, I remain skeptical of managers even as a manager. While I believe managers are an essential part of a scaling organization, I don't believe they have a monopoly on leadership, and I work hard to build other constructs and opportunities in my teams for nonmanagers to effectively lead.

I see things as systems. I reduce all complex things (including humans) into systems. I think in flowcharts. I take great joy in attempting to understand how these systems and flowcharts all fit together. When I see large or small inefficiencies in systems, I like to fix them, with your help.

It is important to me that humans are treated fairly. I believe that most humans are trying to do the right thing, but unconscious bias leads them astray. I work hard to understand and address my biases because I understand their ability to create inequity.

I heavily bias toward action. Long meetings where we are endlessly debating potential directions are often valuable, but I believe starting is the best way to begin learning and make progress. This is not always the correct strategy. This strategy annoys those who like to debate.

I believe in the compounding awesomeness of continually fixing small things. I believe quality assurance is everyone's responsibility and there are bugs to be fixed everywhere...all the time.

I start with an assumption of positive intent for all involved. This has ，
well for me over my career.

*I need you to know that sometimes we are in HIGH ALERT and things will ｇ．
strange.* There is an exception to many of my practices and principles, and that is
when we are in a HIGH ALERT situation. HIGH ALERT conditions usually
involve existential threats to our company. During this time, my usual people,
process, and product protocols are secondary to countering this threat. If it is not
obvious, I will alert you that I am in this state and give you my best guess of
when we'll be done. If I am constantly in this state, something is fundamentally
wrong.

Feedback Protocol

I firmly believe that feedback is at the core of building trust and respect in a
team.

At $COMPANY, there is a formal feedback cycle that occurs twice a year. The
first time we go through this cycle, we'll draft a proposed set of OKRs (*https://
oreil.ly/qEr4R*) for you for the next review period. These are not product or technology OKRs; these are professional growth OKRs just for you. I'll send you
these draft OKRs as well as upward feedback from your team before we meet so
you can review beforehand.

In our face-to-face meeting, we'll discuss and agree on your OKRs for the
next period, and I'll ask for feedback on my performance. At our following
review, the process differs thusly: I'll review you against our prior OKRs, and I'll
introduce new OKRs (if necessary). Rinse and repeat.

Review periods are not the only time we'll exchange feedback. This will be a
recurring topic in our 1:1s. I am going to ask you for feedback in 1:1s regularly. I
am never going to stop doing this, no matter how many times you say you have
no feedback for me.

Disagreement is feedback, and the sooner we learn how to efficiently disagree with each other, the sooner (and more) we'll trust and respect each other.
Ideas don't get better with agreement.

Meeting Protocol

I go to a lot of meetings. I deliberately run with my calendar publicly visible. If
you have a question about a meeting on my calendar, ask me. If a meeting is private or confidential, its title and attendees will be hidden from your view. The
vast majority of my meetings are neither private nor confidential.

My definition of a meeting includes an agenda and/or intended purpose, the appropriate amount of productive attendees, and a responsible party who will be running the meeting to a schedule. If I am attending a meeting, I'd prefer starting on time. If I am running a meeting, I will start that meeting on time. If it's not clear to me why I am in a meeting, I will ask for clarification on my attendance.

If you send me a presentation deck a reasonable amount of time before a meeting, I will read it before the meeting and will have my questions at the ready. If I haven't read the deck, I will tell you.

If a meeting completes its intended purpose before it's scheduled to end, let's give the time back to everyone. If it's clear the intended goal won't be achieved in the allotted time, let's stop the meeting before time is up and determine how to finish the meeting later.

Nuance and Errata

I am an introvert, and that means that prolonged exposure to humans is exhausting for me. Weird, huh? Meetings with three of us are perfect. Three to eight is okay. More than eight, and you will find that I am strangely quiet. Do not confuse my quiet with lack of engagement.

When the 1:1 feels over and there is remaining time, I always have a couple of meaty topics to discuss. This is brainstorming, and the issues are usually front-of-mind hard topics that I am processing. It might feel like we're shooting the s—t, but we're doing real work.

When I ask you to do something that feels poorly defined, you should ask me for both clarification and a call on importance. I might still be brainstorming. These questions can save everyone a lot of time.

Ask assertively, don't tell assertively. When you need to ask me to do something, ask me. I respond incredibly well to ask-assertiveness ("Rands, can you help with X?"). I respond poorly to being told what to do ("Rands, do X.") I have been this way since I was a kid and I probably need therapy.

I can be hyperbolic, but it's almost always because I am excited about the topic. I also swear sometimes. Sorry.

I love to start new things, but I often lose interest when I can mentally see how the thing is going to finish, which might be weeks or months before the thing is actually done. Sorry. I'm getting better at this.

If I am on my phone during a meeting for more than 30 seconds, say something. My attention wanders.

Humans stating opinions as facts are a trigger for me.

Humans who gossip are a trigger for me.

This document is a living, breathing thing and likely incomplete. I update it frequently and would appreciate your feedback.

30

Be Unfailingly Kind

DJ and I play Destiny (*https://www.destinythegame.com*). I've only met DJ once in real life, but most weeks he and I and a dozen or so other regulars are sitting on our respective couches, desks, chairs, and bean bags tackling the various parts of this gorgeous first-person shooter game.

You can play much of Destiny by yourself. There are daily missions on various planets where you can find and kill the bad guys and then collect the loot. There are daily strikes where you are paired with two random strangers to run a slightly harder mission where there is no need for formal communication, just the collective firepower of three players versus one player. Finally, there are raids. These are complex, longer missions requiring multiple people who are actively communicating and coordinating. This means someone—however subtly—needs to lead the group. In my ideal raid, DJ is the leader.

While this chapter is going to talk a lot about Destiny, it's really about leadership. See, in the many hours I've spent listening to DJ walk the raiding group through Venus's Vault of Glass or Crota's End on the Moon, I've learned the power that comes with DJ's leadership style: he's unfailingly kind.

Regarding Colorful Personalities and Opinions

If you've ever read YouTube comments, you know that public spaces on the internet attract humanity's most colorful personalities and opinions. While I completely respect your right to have an opinion, I am not interested in your colorful agenda during my precious downtime. Playing Destiny during my downtime offers me an escape. I need a gorgeous puzzle to solve that involves as little of my daily routine as possible. Often those puzzles require other humans.

Having played many multiplayer games before Destiny, I'm aware that joining a group of strangers from the internet can be problematic. There is the

Never_Stop_Talking player who sees this particular raid as an opportunity to talk about...anything...forever. There is the I_Know_Everything player who is immediately verbally frustrated when the group's level of experience is lower than theirs.

One of the reasons I've written online extensively about Destiny is to find a collection of somewhat like-minded players with roughly the same experience.[1] This experiment was successful, and at any given time there are 20 to 30 players on my friends list. From this list, it's minimal work to cobble together a group to tackle any part of Destiny. Even within this like-minded group, there is still diversity. There are still competing agendas, and differing experiences—and that brings us back to DJ.

Raid Mechanics

To understand the difficulties of DJ's job as a raid leader, you need to understand a bit about raid mechanics. If you start to glaze over when you read the phrase "raid mechanics," please stick with me. My goal here is to explain how you can be a better leader.

To successfully raid, you first need multiple competent, willing humans. Raids often involve more powerful enemies (or "bosses") who need to be conquered in a specific fashion to gain access to raid-exclusive loot. For example, for one encounter in Destiny, the boss must first be hit with massive damage by multiple players at precisely the same time just so another player who is carrying a sword (acquired from another baddie who also must be killed with a coordinated attack) can inflict damage on the boss. Failure to perform this sequence in this precise order results in the quick death of your entire party. It's called a wipe. Oh yeah, you need to perform this entire sword-wielding maneuver multiple times to actually kill this boss.

It's fun. I swear. And there's more.

Six strangers spread across the planet and speaking via headset need to show up at the same time of day and organically anoint a leader whose job it is to quickly determine the relative experience of each stranger, ascertain who needs to know what about the mechanics of this particular raid, and then clearly explain these mechanics. Once the encounter has begun, the raid leader needs to make strategy adjustments in real time based on the performance of the team.

---

1 Yes! I'm still playing. Yes! I'd like to play with you. Join the Destiny Slack by dropping me a note—I'm on the Internet.

These humans show up late. These humans have a variety of experience with first-person shooters and with Destiny. (Even the most experienced humans sometimes screw up during a raid.) These humans have real lives and often need to vanish at a moment's notice. However, these humans are collectively motivated to learn and progress through the game because it gives them joy.

No Worries...

Having run dozens of raids, DJ has learned, and consistently demonstrates, four leadership behaviors:

- He clearly explains the situation. As many times as possible. Calmly.
- He has an insightful answer ready for any question. He's done his research to become an expert in his field.
- Once the raid has begun, he monitors the situation, provides real-time feedback, and updates the other players in a helpful and educational manner.
- In the face of disaster, he never loses composure.

Clear communications, demonstrated expertise, clear and actionable feedback, and even-keeled temperament. I'm describing a set of solid leadership traits here, but I'm not even to the important part. See, I've seen all these behaviors before in a great many humans. What makes DJ unique is that: *he's always this leader.* I've come to expect precisely this behavior out of DJ each time we've played—like clockwork. I aspire to be a good leader, but I have bad days. I slept poorly. I sat in that useless meeting where nothing of substance was contemplated for an hour, and I lost my faith in humanity.

DJ is always this leader. Need to leave a raid after we've been at it unsuccessfully for two hours to be with your family? DJ says, "No worries, we'll find someone else..." Having repeated difficulty fulfilling your role in this part of the raid, which is resulting in multiple wipes? "No worries, let's try a slightly different strategy, okay?" Never played this raid before? Didn't mention this before the raid began? "No worries, I remember my first time playing this. It's fun to learn. Let me walk you through how this works..."

I've played a lot of video games with a lot of humans. I've led and been led by a lot of different people and personalities, but never have I so plainly seen the clear and consistent results of being unfailingly kind. Following DJ's lead, we communicate better, we learn from each other, we celebrate our successes, and we laugh heartily about our failures.

Regarding Jerks

Leadership in a volunteer organization is perhaps the best way to think about leading a raid. You have a set of humans that are hopefully dedicated to a common goal, and that are donating their time in support of this goal. Most volunteer organizations have a far nobler mission than the acquisition of epic loot, but the theory is that when you have a volunteer workforce of people donating their time out of the kindness of their hearts, you see a different leadership approach.

I believe two things. First, an unfailingly kind leadership protocol seems like a solid approach for a volunteer organization. You don't hire your team, and they likely come from diverse backgrounds with different motivations, so your ability to explain and guide is key. Your ability to convey credibility and become the expert as quickly as possible is paramount because volunteers leave...randomly. In the face of disaster, you must remain a calm and focused leader—this leadership trait is essential. Disaster is a strong word, but in a world where volunteers are doing work they are choosing to do rather than work they must do, unexpected situations are the norm.

Second, I believe being unfailingly kind is the best approach for every leadership situation. As you've been reading this chapter, you've probably thought of a leader who is precisely the opposite of what I've described. They're a dictator, a micromanager, a yelling, driven, larger-than-life personality. You might believe they are successful because of these traits, and that might be true, but is that the leader you aspire to be?

Not me.

One for Your Pocket

There are 30 different small things in this book. As we wind down, I'm curious about which ones you picked, and why. Overwhelmed? Don't know where to start? Pick the easiest and start right now. The hard part isn't the choice; it lies in discovering why that small thing is important and how it will make you a better leader.

For me, I've been focused on reliability for the past year. I wanted to make certain that when you asked me to complete a thing, you believed that I would commit without fail. The year before that, I was working on communication in large organizations. What was the most efficient way to communicate with every single human in my team, my organization, my company? Know what? There are lots of different ways to communicate, and the best approach I've found is admitting I'll never have the perfect approach and that I'm always learning.

Meanwhile, there are a handful of leadership principles—small things—that are unchanging and that I forever keep in my pocket. The most important? My default mindset in all situations is a mindset of *kindness*. When you walk into the meeting guns blazing because I screwed up badly? Kindness. *I'm sorry I screwed up.* When I hear that heinous rumor designed to anger humans and foment distrust? Kindness. *Well, that's untrue, but someone is clearly trying to say something important.*

Leadership is an outfit you choose for others to see, and I choose to be unfailingly kind.

Epilogue: The Way
I Heard It Was...

We're a team. There's a mountain that no one has ever climbed before, but you—in your bones—believe we can. More importantly, you can stand in front of us, point at the mountain, and tell us the compelling story of how we're going to climb that impossible peak.

You talk with your hands, you raise your voice at precisely the right times to punctuate your thoughts. Your pauses build tension. You're not talking about yourself, you're talking about all of us and how we are going to collectively achieve this impossible task.

Your story is engaging, but light on specifics. We don't care because we all desire to achieve the impossible and, more importantly, we just love the way you tell this story. We believe you. This belief washes away the perceived need for concrete next steps. We are emotional beings; your manner and delivery have convinced us to follow you on an impossible journey.

This is vision. You are using all your leadership skills to describe a vision.

There is still a mountain to climb. How are we actually going to perform this Herculean feat? Thankfully, we have you. Now you begin to plan.

You start with questions: How big is the mountain? What obstacles are we aware of? Where is the top? What is the best path to climb to the top? Are there alternative paths? How many hikers do we have, and how fit are they? What are their respective strengths and weaknesses? What is the best configuration of humans to perform each task? What contingencies are we going to need to build for unexpected developments while hiking?

It's an endless list of questions, so you first determine which answers are critical, which are important, and which are nice to have. Second, you hand the task of answering many of these questions to humans on your team. You do this by first reminding us of your vision, explaining the relative importance of the questions, and defining when you need to know an answer. Each time, without fail, you finish with *I trust you to do this important thing.*

You learn not just from the answers, but from how the team discovers answers. Their discoveries update your mental model of not only how we're going to achieve this impossible task, but also the abilities and nuances of the humans you will need to depend upon.

Conflicting opinions. Confusing data. Unexpected developments. Interpersonal conflict. We sometimes miss the bliss of the vision and despair. *I'm not sure I can do this.* You respond immediately, "It seems an impossible thing. Of course it's hard, but *we* are going to do this together, and I'll explain how."

And you do.

All of the answers have developed into a draft of a credible plan. You find trusted advisors with whom you test the particulars of the plan. These advisors unabashedly tell you the truth. You eagerly listen to their truth. You iterate. Finally, you stand in front of all of us, describe the vision once more, and then tell us how we'll execute on the plan with a well-defined strategy.

"We are going to climb this mountain. Thanks to all of your hard work, we now have a strategy. We know each part of the climb, how we'll be organized, and how we'll tackle each day." You draw the mountain, you draw the planned trail, and you draw signs along the trail to describe how each step of the climb will go.

We have lots of questions. You eloquently and completely answer our questions, which builds our confidence. We are still scared because no one has climbed this mountain before, but as we stare at the picture we built together we believe it can be done.

This is strategy. You are using all your leadership skills to define a strategy that supports a vision.

We begin the climb.

The execution of the plan, the tactics, is the hardest part, but no one will believe this for a while. We're optimistic, full of energy, and chasing an ambitious, compelling vision. We're laughing, patting ourselves on the back, and climbing. We frequently look at the plan that we've built, read the signs, and follow the directions. Step after step.

As each day passes, we discover small flaws in our plan. Unexpected developments that our strategy did not take into account. We stop, regroup, and share thoughts on how to proceed. You listen, ask questions, and make a quick decision. We nod, satisfied, and keep climbing.

Days pass and we continue to discover the unexpected. The frequency of the unexpected begins to concern a small group of us. You can hear despair and you show up quickly to talk directly to us. You remind us of the vision. You remind us that no one has done this before, for good reason. It's not that other humans weren't smart or organized enough, it was simply that they didn't believe in the impossible. And we do.

Your words and enthusiasm calm some of us, but others will never come back to belief. They will continue to climb, but the magnitude of the task will never seem less than impossible. They will not finish the climb with us.

Disaster strikes. Not just an unexpected development, but a complete and total disastrous surprise. Worse, the disaster shines a light on the simple known fact that this task *is* impossible and our strategy is clearly, woefully flawed. All of us are rattled. Including you. Someone asks, "Should we turn back?" and the deep murmurs of agreement show the degree of despair and disbelief within the team.

This started as tactics. You were using all your leadership skills to execute tactics that supported the strategy to achieve the vision. Now you must use judgment if we are to succeed.

Judgment. The accumulation of all of your experiences into wisdom. Readily accessible, informed inspiration. Judgment isn't just what you rely on to make a decision; judgment tells you when a decision exists. Are we going to stop or continue? What are the costs of each? How much do we risk if we continue? What do we forever lose if we stop? Is now the time to decide?

As you stand in front of us, hearing the echoing murmurs of despair, you make a decision because you are accountable for this journey, and while most believe accountability means responsibility you understand that it means being *required or expected to justify actions and decisions.* Justify to whom? To us. To give account. To tell the tale of why we are here. To justify why we need to complete this impossible task. To make the decision to continue and to explain in understandable detail what changes we'll need to make to achieve our goal.

You make your decision. *We are going to continue.* You explain your decision. *And this is how we'll proceed differently.* You repeat the vision, you repeat the now revised strategy and supporting tactics. You feel you've done this a hundred times, but you'll do it a hundred more before you're done because each human needs a different thing to hold on to at different times in their journey.

Wild enthusiasm is gone. Belief is shaky. Your words can't prevent a few from turning back, but those who stay take a deep breath, remember why they are there, and start climbing again.

Interlude: The Test

How do you interview for leadership skills? I hear this question a lot, and 9 times out of 10 the thoughtful but predictable response is, "Ask them about the last person they let go."

It's a good question because it's not a yes/no question. It's a good question because it begins a discussion involving a complex people situation—but letting someone go is the last step in a very long set of leadership maneuvers. It's an important question, but a more important question is, "Why'd you have to let that person go?" or "What could you have done differently to achieve a different outcome?"

Leadership is a set of principles that you mostly follow. You may have never written them down, but if we sat down over coffee we'd find a few of them in short order. Here are a few of mine:

- I believe that humans should be treated fairly.
- I believe that it is the responsibility of a leader to be painfully reliable.
- I believe that the primary job of a leader is to grow their team.

The first part of this test is to write down your leadership principles on a piece of paper. Just for you. Take 30 minutes. It's important. I'll wait.

Done? Okay, take your list of draft principles, fold it into a neat little square, and tuck it somewhere safe but accessible. I want you to look at it once or twice a day for a week. New principles will arrive. Some will feel less important after a good night of sleep. Give it a week and see what happens to the list.

The second part involves VST+J. That's my rubric for understanding leaders. Vision, Strategy, Tactics + Judgment. Go to a whiteboard (or some other blank surface) and draw this:

	CURRENT	IDEAL
VISION		
STRATEGY		
TACTICS		

You have 100 points to allocate for each column. What's your current relative strength on Vision, Strategy, and Tactics? What would you like it to be, in an ideal world? There is no wrong answer here; this is meant for you to assess how strong you are on these broad sets of leadership attributes defined in our mountain-climbing story. Remember:

Vision

Seeing an impossible objective, defining the broad strokes of how we might achieve it, and selling us on the idea.

Strategy

Breaking down the vision into understandable chunks and defining the concrete steps we'll need to take to meet the chunked individual goals.

Tactics

Unfailingly following each step as described.

Allocate away. (Bonus exercise: have a trusted someone rank you as well, and compare notes. It's illuminating.)

You now have three important pieces of information:

1. A draft of your leadership principles, or simply a list of things that are important to you as a leader.

2. My rubric for how I understand leaders, and an assessment of your strengths and where you'd like to invest.

3. A list of 30 small things to consider. In early drafts of this book, I attempted to map each small thing to Vision, Strategy, and Tactics, but after a few chapters I realized what might be a strategic small thing for one leader might be a tactical one for another. For example, 1:1s, for me, are strategic. I employ 1:1s because I need help building strategy. But 1:1s for you might be tactical. They might be your tactical move to communicate your reliability to the team.

Here's the final piece of work: *use Judgment.* Given your principles and where you want to invest in terms of VST, what are the small things that you want to learn and practice? Why? The justification might feel thin right now. It might just be a feeling. So, as I wrote at the beginning of this book, decide which small things are most relevant for you, perform them every working day for the next three months, and see what you experience and learn.

Small Steps

Climbing. One step at a time.

The first disaster is far behind us. The second one, too. More members of the team have left, but others have now joined because they're inspired by our ambition, and also because it's become well known that we are still climbing.

There are two more disasters ahead of us, but in six short weeks, we'll reach the summit. The impossible will have been achieved. No one believes this right now. We are singularly focused on the task at hand: the act of taking each small step. The most important thing we do is take another small step.

There are no hacks. There are no silver bullets. The way that we are going to achieve this impossible task is by continuing to climb.

Index

Symbols

1:1s
    critical information sharing in, 141
    definition of term, xvii
    giving and requesting feedback in, 74
    increasing value of, 3-4
    Rands user guide, 153
    reading the room, 14
    value of, xiii
    with distributed team members, 91-94
360 reviews, 147-150

A

accountability
    meaning of, 167
    versus responsibility, 47
agendas, 64-66
Anti-Flow, 113-115
Apple, 39-41
art of leadership (see also leadership principles; leadership skills)
    approaches to learning, xv
    definition of term, xiv
Asch conformity tests, 126-128

C

career paths, 117-123
communication (see also feedback)
    cultivating healthy signal networks, 137-141
    dealing with rumors, 125-130
    drafting communication plans, 131-136
    hearing the hard thing, 75, 148
    Rands user guide, 153-157
    saying the hard thing, 73-75
compliments, 69-72
conformity, 126-130
context
    building at meetings, 13
    context acquisition skills, 144
    role in decision making, 10
corporate culture
    company values, 109
    corrosive politics, 66
    dealing with rumors, 125-130
    organizational charts, 87-90
    uncovering, 107-111
corrosive politics, 66
criticism, 75-77, 148-149

D

decision making
    augmented by Anti-Flow, 113-115
    effect of emotional state on, 11, 43-45
    reinforced by Spidey-sense, 17-20
    role of judgement in, 167
    workflow for, 10
delegation, 33-37, 47-50
directors
    challenges faced by, 40
    Small Things, xix
disasters
    learning from, 103-106
    measured approach to, 9, 79-85
    preventing, 96, 131-136
distributed teams, 91-94

E

executives
    challenges faced by, 96, 100
    Small Things, xx

F

fairness, 168
Faux-Zone, 143-146
feedback (see also communication)
    giving and requesting, 73-75
    Rands user guide, 155
    receiving, 75-77
    requesting on a monthly basis, 25-28
    through effective compliments, 71
Five Whys, 83, 83

G

groupthink, 126-128
growth tax, 120

H

half-delegation, 34
high-signal humans, 137-141
honesty
    dealing with rumors, 125-130
    hearing the hard thing, 75-77, 148
    saying the hard thing, 73-75

I

innovation, 101-102
inspiration, 113-115
intuition, 17-20

J

judgment
    applying, 169
    example of, 166-168
    reinforced by Spidey-sense, 17-20

K

kindness, 159-163
Kobayashi Maru management, 131-136

L

leadership principles
    drafting your own, 168-169
    examples of, 168
    fairness, 168
    growing your team, 73, 79-85, 117-123, 168
    kindness, 159-163
    Rands user guide, 154
    reliability, 6, 168
leadership skills
    acting without asking, 99-102
    building, xiv, 18, 59, 147
    context acquisition, 144

dealing with humans, 36
delegation, 47-50
describing strategies, 166
describing visions, 165
detecting nonsense, 128
interviewing for, 168
reading human beings, 2
reliability, 161
saying the hard thing, 73-77

M

managers
    avoiding the New Manager Death Spiral, 33-37
    essential skills for, 2
    Small Things, xix
Meeting Historians, 63
meetings
    avoiding Meeting Blur, 5
    building context, 13
    distributed meetings, 91-94
    increasing value of, 3-4
    instructive curiosity in, 15
    Rands user guide, 155
    reading the room, 14
    well-run staff meetings, 61-67
mentors, 147-151
meritocracy, 117-123
micromanagement, 15
The Must List, 55

N

Netscape, 1-2
New Manager Death Spiral, 33-37

O

objectives and key results (OKRs), 155

offer letters, 58
onboarding, 81-85
1:1s
    critical information sharing in, 141
    definition of term, xvii
    giving and requesting feedback in, 74
    increasing value of, 3-4
    Rands user guide, 153
    reading the room, 14
    value of, xiii
    with distributed team members, 91-94
organizational charts, 87-90

P

patience, 43-45
performance reviews
    checklist for, 25-28
    preparing for, 21-24
perspective, 43-45
politics, 66
problem solving, 113-115
productivity
    state of busy, 143-146
    time-saving practices, 29-32
professional growth
    encouraging, 25-28
    finding a mentor, 147-151
    performance reviews, 25-28
    questionnaire for assessment, 21-24

R

Rands
    Rands Information Practices, 29-32
    randsinrepose.com weblog, xvi
    use of name, xvi
    user guide, 153-157
reading the room, 14

recognition, 69-72

recruitment, 51-59, 82-85

reliability
    as a leadership principle, 161, 168
    avoiding Meeting Blur, 5

remote workers, 91-94

respect
    building, xiii
    demonstrating, 16

responsibility, versus accountability, 47

Rule of 3 and 10, 80

rumors, 125-130

S

signal networks, 137-141

Slack, 95-96

Small Things
    for directors, xix
    for executives, xx
    for managers, xix
    how to use, xv
    selecting one to start, 162

Spidey-sense, 17-20

staff meetings, 61-67

strategy
    definition of term, 169
    example of, 165-166

stress, root cause of, 6

T

tactics
    definition of term, 169
    example of, 166-167

teams
    allowing others to change your mind,
      33-37

    assessing required oversight, 50
    building diverse, 36
    building healthy with compliments,
      69-72
    building productive, 103-106
    building with 1:1s, xiii
    dealing with performance issues, 19
    dealing with rumors, 125-130
    distributed teams, 91-94
    encouraging honesty in, 73-77
    growing, 79-85, 117-123, 168
    onboarding new members, 81
    organizational charts depicting, 87-90
    recruiting team members, 51-59

time management
    reserving time to build things, 143-146
    time-saving practices, 29-32
    unstructured time, 113-115

trust
    building teams that trust themselves,
      104-106
    building through delegation, 34, 47-50
    building with 1:1s, xiii
    building with feedback, 73-77

V

videoconferencing, 91-94

vision
    definition of term, 169
    example of, 165

Vision, Strategy, Tactics + Judgment (VST
    +J), 168-169

Z

the Zone, 113

About the Author

Michael Lopp is a veteran Silicon Valley–based engineering leader who builds both people and product at historic companies such as Slack, Borland, Netscape, Palantir, Pinterest, and Apple. When he's not deeply worrying about staying relevant, he writes about backpacks, bridges, humans, and leadership at the popular blog, Rands in Repose (*https://randsinrepose.com*). He currently works at Apple. This is the way.

Michael has written two other books. His first book *Managing Humans*, 3rd Edition (Apress, 2016) is a popular guide to the art of engineering leadership and clearly explains that while you will be rewarded for what you build, you will only be successful because of your people. His second book, *Being Geek* (O'Reilly, 2010) is a career handbook for geeks and nerds alike.

Michael rides gravel bikes, wonders about semicolons, drinks red wine, and tries to understand how forests work amongst the redwoods of Northern California because curiosity is how you grow.

Colophon

The cover image is by Susan Thompson. The cover fonts are Guardian Sans and Gilroy. The text font is Scala Pro and the heading font is Benton Sans.